...S IN
MEDICINE,
DENTISTRY and
MENTAL HEALTH

CAREERS IN
MEDICINE, DENTISTRY and MENTAL HEALTH

Loulou Brown

eighth edition

**KOGAN
PAGE**

First published in 1981
Second edition 1985
Third edition 1988
Fourth edition 1989
Fifth edition 1992
Sixth edition 1994
Seventh edition 1996
Eighth edition 2000

Kogan Page Limited
120 Pentonville Road
London N1 9JN

British Library Cataloguing in Publication Data

A CIP record for this book is available from the British Library.

ISBN 0 7494 3390 6

Typeset by Jean Cussons Typesetting, Diss, Norfolk
Printed and bound in Great Britain by Clays Ltd, St Ives plc

Contents

1 Introduction

Is this the Job for You?

☐ Are you doing science rather than arts A-levels?

☐ Do you like finding out how things work?

☐ Are you physically fit?

☐ Do you like hard work?

☐ Do you care for people?

☐ Are you a good timekeeper?

☐ Are you quick on your feet?

☐ Do you like being with people?

☐ Do you like solving problems?

☐ Do you have a sense of humour?

If you've answered yes to all these questions, you should think about a career in medicine, dentistry or mental health.

This book draws together career opportunities across the whole field of health care. It is intended for people whose educational background equips them to take a course which will qualify them to practise independently – for instance, as a doctor, dentist, psychologist or osteopath. This means you will probably have to fulfil the requirements for university entrance and, particularly for entry to medical and dental schools, be reasonably confident of getting good A-level results. It also means that you must be willing to spend a considerable number of years in training, as a period of postgraduate study or training is usually a requirement.

Both the undergraduate and postgraduate aspects of training are dealt with and, for this reason, the information should be useful both to sixth-formers and to students who are making decisions about their future careers. Because the choice is wide, these decisions can be difficult, so the main factors influencing choice have been identified and are related to the actual experience of people working in various settings and disciplines. This is done through a series of case studies, conversations with people who were chosen because they represent a wide spectrum of interests and opinions. The views expressed serve to give a picture of the diversity of opportunities available.

This book does not outline many jobs below graduate level. Details of job opportunities in the Health Service for school leavers are available in other Kogan Page titles.

Medicine

Much of the book is about doctors: how to become one and how to decide what type of doctor you want to be. The training structure is complex and although extensive explanatory literature is available to all medical students, this is very factual in its approach and not always helpful with the problems of actually making a choice. Personal accounts in the form of case studies seem more relevant. What are the rewards and pressures, both in training and in subsequent practice? Where do people feel they have made mistakes? What considerations are uppermost when people decide to work in one area rather than another?

Medicine used to be thought of as a male preserve and to some extent this attitude still prevails. For this reason, it is important that women should know what their position within the profession is likely to be in advance. Although there is now no barrier to women becoming students, the system, particularly as regards postgraduate training, is in fact discriminatory, in that it takes no account of possible family commitments. Within hospitals, women predominate in the 'unpopular' specialties. These also tend to be concerned with personal and social problems rather than with technological treatment procedures. Whether women tend to be temperamentally more attracted to this kind of work, or settle for it because it is accessible to them, is an open question. But it cannot be denied that, in a competitive field with little provision for the part-time jobs that women often need, there is still little incentive to create part-time posts in popular areas where plenty of full-time applicants are available.

Dentistry

Dentistry is, overall, less of a competitive jungle than medicine, and has the advantage of a slightly shorter training period. Career opportunities are not as diverse as they are in medicine, but general practice, where most dentists are employed, offers a very independent working situation. Although you will be bound, to some extent, by financial considerations, you will have the freedom to develop your own ideas and style of working and – an important consideration for women – be able to set your own working hours.

Alternative medicine

Alternative medicine describes treatment given through therapies that operate without recourse to pharmacological drugs. There are many such therapies in existence and to practise them you will need the technical skill particular to each one and some degree of background medical knowledge, depending on the subject area. The important feature common to alternative medicine is that treatment is given holistically, that is, about the whole person. You have to be in sympathy with this method of treating illness if you are going to work in this field.

Mental health

Mental health care is the meeting point of the health, social, and education services and people can come to this work via any of these disciplines. The very fact that it demands an all-round view of the patient is its attraction for many people. New moves to create more provision at the early stages of illness are gradually leading to the growth of interesting jobs, within the community as well as in the more traditional hospital settings. It is as well to note, however, that training is a lengthy process in this field, as relevant work experience and a course of professional training must follow a first degree.

The first aim of all people with a responsibility for any form of health care has to be to improve the well-being of their patients, but there are many opinions as to how this is best achieved. Frequently there are changes in emphasis, both in actual methods of treatment and in the organization of the services providing it. New research gives rise to new approaches. Some of the issues currently involved are discussed, along with descriptions of the work areas. Everyone involved in medicine will need to have a strong, personal ideology for the basis of his or her work if it is to extend beyond the technical limits of professional expertise and become an appropriate personal and social service

The publishers would like to thank all those who took the trouble to answer their letters, supply information and comment on the text. Wherever possible, we have used information coming from primary sources, that is, from professional organizations, examining bodies and those working in the field. When we received no satisfactory reply to our requests for information we were forced to turn to secondary sources.

2 Basic medical training

Applying for a course

Selection for interview to a college is made on the strength of an application submitted through the Universities and Colleges Admissions Service (UCAS) – see p 85. You should consult *The UCAS Handbook* for the relevant year of entry: this will provide details of the admissions procedure and how to apply. Note that all applications for medical courses must reach UCAS by no later than 15 October for entry in the following year. A maximum of four choices may be made for courses that lead to a professional qualification in medicine, that is, courses that are coded by UCAS as follows: A100, A101, A103, A104 and A106 – refer to UCAS's *A Student's Guide to Entry in Medicine*. Prospective students are strongly advised to obtain prospectuses of the universities, schools and colleges in which they are interested before making their application, as courses and entrance requirements vary.

Entrance requirements

Many universities require a GCSE (or equivalent) pass in English language. If you are applying for a place at an Oxford or Cambridge college, please note that you cannot apply to both universities in the same admissions year. If, however, you are already a graduate, you can bypass UCAS and apply direct to the particular college of your choice. Some institutions will waive entrance requirements in the case of mature students. Medical colleges and contact points are listed in Chapter 9, pp 85–95. A-level or other requirements and length of study are given after the addresses.

Each medical school is attached both to a university and to a hospital or hospital group. Applicants are usually required to be between the ages of 18 and 30 at the time their studies begin, and at some medical schools the upper age limit can be as low as 25. Competition for medical school places is very keen, with deans usually giving priority to school leavers starting their first university courses. Very few places are therefore available for mature students. Official entry requirements are three A levels at either grade A or grade B in chemistry and other science subjects. Physical science may be an acceptable alternative to physics and/or chemistry.

In 1996, 52 per cent of the intake to medical schools was female and women doctors now make up 31 per cent of the hospital medical workforce in England compared to 25 per cent in 1986. There still seems to be a tendency for schools to recruit a large number of students from families with medical backgrounds, and some schools will only take applicants who make them their first choice.

Scottish applicants to Scottish medical schools are accepted on their results in their SCEs. After taking SCEs, applicants are generally required to study for an additional year and to pass the Scottish Certificate of Sixth Year Studies.

Tuition fees for 2000 are £1,025. They will be more for students starting in 2001. Check with UCAS.

Note that the Department of Health has recommended that medical and dental students should be immunized against Hepatitis B before starting training.

The interview

If you are asked for an interview, you will already have done very well as at least two-thirds of the applicants will already have been rejected. Try not to worry too much; remember that it will not last long (half an hour at most). The interviewers are looking to see if you are committed and interested, and at the same time trying to imagine if you would be a good student and, eventually, a good doctor. You will probably be asked why you want to be a doctor and what you think you might like to specialize in, what interests you have and what work experience you've had so far. At the end of the interview you will almost certainly be asked whether you have any questions to ask the interviewers. Do try to ask at least one question; this makes you look alert and motivated.

Pre-medical (1st MB)

There are some opportunities for people who have taken unacceptable subjects at A level, or equivalent, but who are otherwise academically well qualified, to take a first MB course in basic science subjects. Entry requirements are similar to those for university courses generally, but some evidence of the study of sciences, either at GCSE or A level, is usually required. This will qualify them to apply for further medical training, but these courses are rare. Graduate candidates normally require a first or upper second class honours degree.

Course structure

The basic medical course lasts for five years and can last for six years for students who take an extra year to qualify for a BSc (at Cambridge a BA) in Medical Sciences, or for those who take an intercalated degree course.

Until very recently, basic medical training comprised an unvaried, rigid structure that was the same in all schools. Most medical schools, however, have now adopted a far more innovative, individual and integrated approach to teaching medicine, following the recommendations published by the General Medical Council in 1993 which gave an impetus to medical schools to provide a new style of medical education. For example, the University of Leeds starts with a first aid course and a short introduction to cell and tissue biology. This is followed by the more traditional study of biology, anatomy, biochemistry and physiology. Subsequently, behavioural sciences, communication skills and information technology are studied. St Bartholemew's and the Royal London have an integrated course designed around body systems. University College London's course begins with studying the structure and function of the human body and then focuses on integrated systems, structural and developmental human biology, medical statistics and biometry and the chemistry of the cell and genetics. Although more integrated, some courses are more systems-based while others concentrate more on learning about clinical problems. The traditional course, which is still taught in some medical schools, is divided into two parts: the second MB or pre-clinical period, and the clinical period. For the first two years students learn basic medical sciences. Studies during this time include pathology, physiology, pharmacology, biochemistry and anatomy (which involves dissection of the human body). Some medical schools teach psychology and medical sociology as ancillary subjects. For this part of the course, students will work in the ordinary university terms and the work will be mainly lecture and laboratory based. Whatever the course, there is much more emphasis placed on self-directed teaching and problem-solving rather than simply memorizing facts by rote in lectures.

Whatever medical school you go to, you will be beset with exams. By the end of the second year, you should have passed your second MB examination. At this point most universities encourage students of ability to intercalate an extra year studying a single basic medical subject to honours-degree level. At Oxford and Cambridge, the intercalated year is compulsory.

From the third year onwards, increasing amounts of time are spent in clinical teaching settings and less time in the medical school. The period is spent mainly in teaching hospitals and involves observation of patients and of the doctors dealing with them. The field of studies is wide and includes clinical method, which is the study of finding out information about patients and their illnesses; pathology, which is the academic study of disease; and the application of these two studies to the various specialties. These are the 55 specialist areas of medical and surgical knowledge and practice from which, eventually, each student will have to choose in deciding on a career. For information about the specialties, contact the Royal Colleges (Chapter 9 pp 92–94).

Experience comes from attachment to 'firms', or medical teams, for eight- to ten-week periods. Some firms are general medicine or surgery; others are more specialized. Students move from firm to firm during the last three years of training, and lectures, demonstrations and discussions back up the course. They become familiar with working in hospital wards, get their first introduction to patients and learn the techniques of making physical examinations and obtaining the patients' medical histories. The role assigned to students within the hospital is very humble. They will have many routine tasks to perform, will find themselves being deferential to members of staff, and may generally feel unappreciated. There is also a two-month period in the final year, known as the 'elective', which may be spent, within reason, as each student chooses. Many people take this as an opportunity to go abroad and experience medical work in a Third World country. Others choose to contribute to a research project. Grants are not generally available for the elective, but most medical schools have some sources of funding to help students who wish to go abroad.

During their last three years of training, students are expected to work for periods in a full hospital schedule, including some night duties, and will have four weeks' holiday each year. At the end of this period, the final examinations are taken. These are qualifying examinations but do not yet confer the right to practise. This right is only conferred by registration with the General Medical Council after a further pre-registration year of hospital work.

Life as a medical student

Medical students can find themselves isolated from other people, although this may be less of a problem in medical schools attached to universities. Medical schools tend not to have the range of societies and social groups to be found in the wider setting of a university and for some people this can be limiting (one person spoken to described social life at her medical school as being composed of rugger, beer and Christian Union!). The pressure of work is greater than that for other students, creating the need to concentrate almost entirely on the prescribed area of study, and medics may find they have little or no time to indulge in activities that are more social and in the exchange of ideas. On the bonus side, however, the work is extremely interesting, teaching in most medical schools is of a high standard, and there is the satisfying feeling of pursuing a clear objective.

Grants and loans

For the first four years of study, support for students on under-graduate medical courses is on the same basis as for other higher education students. The Department of Health provides support for the full cost of tuition fees in year 5 of the medical course and beyond. Students also receive means-tested NHS bursaries for year 5 and beyond towards the cost of their maintenance and will be eligible for student loans for the balance of their maintenance costs during these years. Mature students who already have a first degree are likely to face considerable financial problems, as local education authorities have no obligation to support students on further degree courses. Medical schools increasingly insist on a financial guarantee before considering mature candidates. (For further details consult the Educational Grants Advisory Service (see p 85) or the British Medical Association Education Trust (see p 86), or other institutions that provide financial support for medics.)

During the clinical years when students must support themselves for longer than the usual 30 weeks of university terms, additional allowances are made. Most medical schools have various scholarships for which there is open competition. These do not usually amount to much money, but they can help, and they sometimes enable a student to finance a special project.

The pre-registration year

After qualifying, all doctors' paths are the same for one year. They have to work under supervision as a house officer (houseman) in general hospitals. At this time, they have a salary and a set role in the hierarchy of hospital life. When they have completed this year satisfactorily, they can be fully registered with the General Medical Council.

The pre-registration year is usually divided between two six-month posts, one as house physician and one as house surgeon. This should give the young doctor a considerable range of experience from which to make the necessary choices for a future career.

Conditions of work

Life as a house officer is hard. In spite of concerns raised by junior doctors and the Department of Health's agreement to limit the hours worked by junior doctors to no more than 72 hours per week, it is very likely that for the foreseeable future junior doctors will often be working up to, or sometimes in excess of, 80 hours per week. The reduction in hours is being phased in, but rather more slowly than was originally anticipated. There are long periods of 'on call' duties, especially at nights and over weekends. Hospital work has become more acute over the past 10 years. In the past, junior doctors spent a lot of 'on call' time sleeping or relaxing; this, however, is no longer possible.

Although much of the work will be interesting and rewarding, there is a good deal of routine clerical work to be got through, and you will generally be the person on hand for the more run-of-the-mill tasks. You will receive four weeks' holiday a year, with a salary ranging from £21,535 to £26,380 (2000), with extra payments for out-of-hours work.

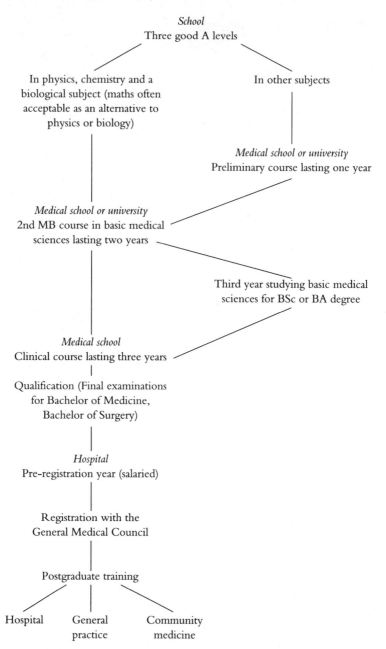

Figure 2.1   Traditional training routes to registration and subsequent career choices

Case Study

A young doctor remembers his pre-registration year as a house officer

It's hard work and very demanding, but it feels good to be doing something useful after being a student and feeling rather superfluous. Having a recognized role is nice, too. The actual work entails being in the hospital from nine until six each day, with one half-day off each week. In addition you are on call every third night and third weekend. The weekends are the worst – by Sunday evening you feel pretty awful.

I worked on just one or two wards and had the care of a group of about 20 to 30 patients. This meant seeing them every day, monitoring their progress and talking to them and their relatives – you are the person who has the time for this, though not always enough of it. Otherwise, your time is spent chasing up investigations and getting ready for the week's high spot – the consultant's ward round. I found the day-to-day contact with the patients satisfying and working on the same wards you get to know the staff well, so the relationships can be quite good.

Sometimes you feel like a dogsbody. There's a lot of clerical work, form filling and so forth, and chasing around, especially in a large teaching hospital.

In my medical post I also worked in outpatient clinics and while working in surgery I assisted at operations. Often this means long hours on one's feet in the theatre when all you might be doing is holding back pieces of skin so that the consultant can operate. That's very tiring. But I did get to do a few minor operations – removing bumps, appendixes and so forth, and I found that satisfying. I think the pay is reasonable – especially as you have no time to spend it except during your four weeks' holiday!

Qualities required

Being a medical student is physically, intellectually and emotionally demanding. During your studies, you will have to absorb an enormous volume of knowledge, and work long hours in physically demanding conditions. As soon as you qualify you will be thrown in at the deep end as far as human relationships are concerned. You will have seen from the case study that the young hospital doctor has the primary personal contact with patients. This means that you will often be required to sort out patients' problems and fears about their illnesses, as well as dealing with worried relatives. You will have to present a confident and reassuring manner while still remaining in a subordinate position in the hospital hierarchy.

The length of training involved should not be underestimated. After the six or seven years described in this chapter, which brings most people well into their mid-20s, doctors must still pursue further postgraduate training before they can become fully independent in their chosen branch of medicine.

Finding a pre-registration post

Although the pre-registration year is part of the basic medical training process, allocation to a post is not automatic. Most medical schools operate a 'matching plan' similar to that used by UCAS, by which the wishes of graduates and the needs of consultants are matched as far as possible. Nevertheless, difficulties can arise if you want to gain experience in an unusual sphere.

Most approved pre-registration posts are in general or district hospitals in the area in which the medical school is situated. It is not possible to obtain a post at a specialist hospital, as they do not usually employ doctors in house officer grades.

In each medical school there will be a staff member who has the responsibility for organizing allocation to pre-registration posts.

Registration

If you wish to qualify as a doctor in the UK, you must first obtain, by examination, a primary qualification that confers a title to registration under the Medical Act. You are then entitled to apply for provisional registration, and after satisfactorily completing one year as a student house officer in approved hospitals you are eligible to apply for full registration. The General Medical Council keeps the Register of all qualified medical practitioners.

3 The hospital doctor

Working for the National Health Service

Roughly 25 per cent of doctors work in hospitals and more than 95 per cent of newly graduated doctors begin their careers working in a hospital within the National Health Service (NHS). Although some NHS hospitals take private patients, it is up to individual doctors (usually only at consultant level) to decide whether they are willing to take on private work. Working for the Health Service is, therefore, the norm and it is NHS hospital work that is described in this chapter.

A hospital doctor is likely to see a patient for a short time, deal with the problem presented, and then proceed to another problem with another patient. It is the problem presented rather than the individual as a whole that is the major concern of the hospital doctor.

Training posts

The first four grades of hospital medical staff are known as training posts. These are house officer (houseman), senior house officer (SHO), registrar and senior registrar. They represent a set hierarchy of responsibility and, while moving through them, all doctors work under the supervision of the consultant who also has responsibility for their postgraduate training. The atmosphere is very competitive, each post being held for a specified time after which the doctor must seek another. It is only at consultant level that doctors are considered fully trained and fully independent. Staff-grade doctors and associated specialists have permanent appointments but are not fully independent.

Postgraduate training

While working in training posts, doctors combine their working life with postgraduate study and further examinations. They move around the various specialties in posts of 6 or 12 months' duration, and have to maintain a demanding working pace. The pressure will ease a little at the higher grades but only somewhat; the pressures of work and examinations will continue to be high for some time.

Postgraduate training is in the nature of an apprenticeship. All hospital doctors eventually work in one of 55 specialties, which they learn on the job with the aid of any optional short courses that may be available. Higher examinations are necessary for promotion. These are not university degrees but professional awards of the Royal Colleges of the various specialties. Most are taken in two parts and all have a written and practical component. The pass rate of these examinations is very low, sometimes only 10 to 15 per cent. It is therefore common for exams to be taken more than once.

The general pattern of postgraduate training consists of about three years of general training in areas relevant to the eventual specialty, followed by four years of specialist training, usually in senior registrar posts. Sometimes, both parts of the examination of the Royal College concerned are taken during the general training period and act as a qualification for admission to specialist training. Sometimes it is possible to take Part 2 of the examination after embarking on specialist training. Each Royal College has a Specialist Training Authority responsible for the overall supervision of postgraduate medical training and for awarding the UK Certificate of Completion of Specialist Training (CCST). This demonstrates that a doctor has completed a training programme that meets the requirements of the EC Medical Directive to a standard compatible with independent practice and is eligible for appointment as a consultant. For further details of postgraduate training, contact either the British Medical Association (p 85) or the Department of Postgraduate Medicine and Dentistry (p 86).

Part-time training

The demands of the postgraduate training period can be particularly difficult for some women who may have commitments to young children during this time. Opportunities for part-time training are limited and depend largely on the exercising of personal initiative. Hospital doctors in training can apply to job-share a full-time establishment post, or a part-time post, but for this they will need the approval of the relevant Royal College and the funding authority. Details of these part-time training schemes are available from postgraduate deans, clinical tutors and employing authorities. For those who are unable to work at least half-time there is the doctors' retainer scheme, which allows doctors to work a maximum of one day a week and attend a minimum of seven educational sessions a year. The Medical Women's Federation (see p 86) has a network of careers advisers throughout the UK who can provide information, advice and counselling for members wishing to work either full- or part-time. The Federation also publishes a journal *Medical Woman* that from time to time carries articles on careers, including part-time opportunities, in different specialties.

Specialties

The tendency towards specialization is increasing all the time. It is impossible to list all the specialties and sub-specialties within hospital work. For practical purposes, however, these can be divided into groups that can be aligned with the various colleges: surgery, medicine, pathology, psychiatry, anaesthetics, radiology, obstetrics and gynaecology. Apart from psychiatry, which is dealt with in Chapter 8, this chapter is concerned with all the specialties mentioned above. For details of the Royal Colleges and contact points, see Chapter 9, p 85–95.

Although there are areas of overlap where people from one discipline work in cooperation with those from another, the specialties are clearly defined, not only in terms of the interests and skills they require but also in terms of the personalities and temperaments of the people they are likely to attract. The responsibilities and rewards of each are very different and many people, while still undergraduates, will find themselves drawn to one area more than another.

Newly qualified doctors are well advised to choose their specialty early in their working life. Your choice will depend not only on your personal interests but also on the general conditions of work and career pattern you have in mind.

Working conditions

The main factor influencing working conditions is the nature of the illness being dealt with and the likely incidence of emergency cases. Someone working in orthopaedic surgery (that is, dealing with broken and injured bones), for instance, is likely to have far more out-of-hours work than a dermatologist, who treats skin diseases. Both will have their set times of night and weekend duty but the working pace this entails will usually be quite different.

Women doctors are more heavily concentrated in less 'acute' specialties, such as radiology, anaesthetics or geriatrics, because 'on call' commitment (that is, the time spent either at home or in the hospital awaiting emergencies) is less. This allows women to combine a position of responsibility with childcare, housework and other functions society still deems are women's, but not men's, roles.

There is a great disparity in the career prospects of different specialties. There are popular and unpopular ones; those that have a high growth rate and those that do not. In general, surgical specialties have a low growth rate and correspondingly high competition for jobs. Most medical specialties are popular and therefore relatively difficult to get into, but career prospects

Medicine

Audiological medicine	General medicine
Cardiology	Geriatric medicine
Clinical genetics	Infectious diseases
Clinical neurophysiology	Medical oncology
Clinical pharmacology and therapeutics	Nephrology
Clinical physiology	Neurology
Dermatology	Nuclear medicine
Diseases of the chest	Paediatrics
Endocrinology	Rheumatology
Gastroenterology	Venereology

Pathology

Blood transfusion	Histopathology
Chemical pathology	Immunopathology
General pathology	Microbiology
Haematology	Neuropathology

Psychiatry

Child and adolescent psychiatry	Mental handicap
Forensic psychiatry	Mental illness (adult)
Psychotherapy	

Surgery

Accident and emergency	Ophthalmology
Cardiothoracic surgery	Paediatric surgery
Ear, nose and throat	Plastic surgery
General surgery	Traumatic and orthopaedic surgery
Neurosurgery	Urology

Other

Anaesthetics	Radiology
Gynaecology and obstetrics	Radiotherapy

Table 2.1   Main hospital specialties

in geriatric medicine, dermatology and medical audiology are good. Pathology, the study of disease, also offers good career prospects.

Surgery

Surgery is about operations. Surgeons tend to have a practical view of illness. Their task is specific: they have to use their skill in a very tangible way to solve a particular problem. Often their interest is restricted to the area of the patient that is being operated on, and this may well be at the expense of an all-round view of the patient as a person. Some emotional distancing may be necessary in surgery where unpleasant mutilations often have to be performed. On the other hand, the surgeon will assume complete responsibility for each patient before, during and after an operation. In no other branch of medicine is one person so directly responsible for the outcome of the treatment given.

Surgery is very definitely not a part-time profession and at the present time (2000) in the UK only 2 per cent of surgeons are women.

Case Study

A talk with a consultant general surgeon

Surgery is very satisfying – I feel immensely privileged being able to do it. I have a pride in being a craftsman and using my skill in a useful way. I like the independent working situation, the personal responsibility. I would not do a major operation if I were unable to follow up on the subsequent progress of the patient. Not many of us are keen on the team concept of working, though that obviously comes into it to some extent.

As a surgeon, you have to get used to the fact of death. I think this is why surgeons tend to be a bit extrovert, with not too much insight. Too much soul-searching is bad for the patient and for you. Surgery is not, on the whole, a terribly intellectual pursuit. If you have difficult diagnostic problems you can ask a physician for help. This means that you can keep on doing it. There are not the problems of keeping up with the younger people that there are in other areas. I do most of my 'keeping up' through conferences and meetings which I find more useful than reading.

I think it's a pity that the present training structure seems to be keeping women out of surgery. It is not practically possible to have part-time posts in surgery because of the personal commitment to patients, and many women during the training period can only work part-time. What we need is an alternative training scheme beginning at the age of 35 or so, but I doubt that would be acceptable on economic grounds.

Medicine

Medicine is about care for patients who do not need operations. Although there are many routine methods of investigation and treatment, the task of the physician is usually less specific than that of the surgeon. Where there is an element of doubt, doctors have to rely to a large extent on their personal judgement both for interpreting the information available and in deciding treatment.

There are many different specialties within medicine. Some deal with patients who have acute illnesses, for whom it is usually possible to suggest some well-defined curative treatment. Others deal with people who have long-term disorders and need periodic hospital care for the management of their illnesses. In such cases, there is a lasting commitment to the patient, who may never, in any sense, be 'cured'. In all situations, doctors work in a team and can rely on specialist help from colleagues in other disciplines where appropriate.

Paediatrics

Paediatrics is general medicine as applied to children. It covers the whole age range from the neo-natal period up to puberty, and sometimes beyond. In hospitals, doctors are dealing only with new-born or sick children but they also need to know about the development of healthy children and the facilities available to them in the community. For this reason it is a good idea, during the training period, to get away from the hospital for a time and work in a child health clinic or development assessment centre.

One of the special features of paediatrics is that the patients often cannot tell you what is wrong. Young children, particularly, are very much a diagnostic challenge, and communication in this case has to be through the parents or the adults close to them.

In paediatrics, the working pace is varied and unpredictable and there is likely to be much out-of-hours work. Nevertheless, it is a popular specialty and competition for jobs is high.

Case Study

A paediatrician outlines her work

When I was working in surgery as a house officer, I disliked the time spent waiting for the patients to be anaesthetized and I found the diagnostic challenge of medical patients much more rewarding than being a technician, just operating. Originally I thought of doing medicine as a preparation for specializing in pathology, but as a student I did my pathology after I'd done some paediatrics and I found I missed the children. At that point I decided to become a paediatrician.

I didn't know if I could cope, emotionally, with very sick children, so I went to a post at the Hospital for Sick Children at Great Ormond Street. Very few children actually die in district hospitals, whereas at Great Ormond Street there can be as many as 500 deaths a year, so this was a good test. Once I was involved, I didn't find this a burden at all. Of course, I got very upset – I still do – when children died. But often, sadly, these deaths can be a relief after long and difficult illnesses. It is only the occasional ones involving previously healthy children or accident cases that are really difficult to accept.

After my pre-registration year, I did three senior house officer jobs, one in general medicine and the others in obstetrics and gynaecology, and neonatology. Then I had a two-year period as a registrar that was divided between two posts, one at a general hospital and the other at a teaching hospital, when I did general paediatrics and more neonatology. After this I got my present job, and spent the first two years of it doing research. I think research is an important part of training as it can take you out of the hospital or into allied areas such as obstetrics and gynaecology and child psychiatry, and give you a broader view.

I like the atmosphere of paediatric wards. Children are much nicer as patients, and when they are better they will let you know. They have no self-awareness to hinder their recovery. They don't think of themselves as sick or feel sorry for themselves. In fact, they have a much greater pain tolerance than adults but lose this as they grow up. They are much happier too – paediatric wards are always noisier and more chaotic than others, and very friendly places.

It *can* be hard work, though. Children, and particularly babies, don't respect the time of day or night. Technically, too, you have to be very skilled. You are working on a smaller scale and you can't be clumsy. But the atmosphere on the wards and the fact that you are working with patients as individuals as well as with the whole family makes the job very special for me.

Pathology

Pathology is the study of disease, of its causation and effect on the body. Pathologists help clinicians with diagnosis and can be involved with making recommendations for treatment and assessing the subsequent progress of patients. Most of the work is laboratory based and, though there may be some contact with patients, this is usually in an advisory capacity and in cooperation with the doctors treating them.

There is a whole range of laboratory techniques used in pathology and these fall under four main groupings:

◆ *Chemical pathology*. This involves the measurement of chemical substances in the body, such as salts, hormones etc. The pathologist's job is to decide which tests are most appropriate in individual cases and to interpret the results in the light of knowledge obtained about the patient.

◆ *Haematology*. This is the study of blood. The haematologist measures such things as the number and character of blood cells, and is concerned with bone marrow, which is involved in the production of blood. Of all branches of pathology, haematology affords the most contact with patients, as it is vital in the diagnosis and treatment of the various forms of anaemia and of leukaemia. Haematologists have the care of patients with these illnesses and make clinical decisions about their treatment.

◆ *Histopathology*. Histopathologists examine the structure and abnormalities of macroscopic and microscopic body tissues. The work is mainly of two kinds: first, the examination of tissues from living patients for diagnostic purposes; second, post-mortem examination to determine the cause of death when this has not otherwise been established.

Some pathologists can, at times, be called on to carry out post-mortem examinations at the request of a coroner, and a few are regularly involved in forensic work of this kind.

◆ *Microbiology*. This is the study of disease-producing microorganisms. The microbiologist examines swabs and other samples of body products in order to isolate and identify the organisms which are causing the trouble. Tests are then carried out on the organisms so that suitable treatment can be recommended. In the light of the test findings, the microbiologist is able to advise, for example, which antibiotics will be effective. The work can also involve investigating outbreaks of infectious disease and identifying the strain of bacteria concerned in order to bring an epidemic under control.

Working conditions

Most pathologists work in laboratories attached to hospitals but some are employed in other organizations, such as the DSS-financed Public Health Laboratory Service (for details see p 86). Laboratory technicians are employed to carry out the many tests that are performed; pathologists advise on the carrying out of the tests and then interpret the results. They also provide the liaison between the laboratory staff and the doctors using their services.

As this is an area where knowledge is increasing fast there is a tremendous volume of new information to be absorbed. The work is obviously most attractive to people who are interested in the scientific aspects of medicine and wish to work in the calmer, nine-to-five world of the laboratory rather than the hurly-burly of night duties and clinical decision taking.

Case Study

A microbiologist talks about his job

Michael *is 31 and employed as an assistant microbiologist (equivalent to senior registrar grade) by the Public Health Laboratory Service.*

I qualified seven years ago and, after 18 months of houseman [house officer] jobs, mainly in general medicine, I decided to go into pathology. I spent the next two years doing a bit of everything before I began to specialize in microbiology. Then I did a year's full-time course at the School of Hygiene and Tropical Medicine in London to get an MSc in medical microbiology. After that I came into my present job. Even as a student I was attracted to the scientific side of things, so I suppose pathology was an obvious choice. The main danger I see is that it's easy to specialize too much, so that eventually you might be working on only one organism. Then the work becomes very enclosed and academic and it's easy to lose a sense of its practical application. I try to avoid too much specialization by doing small projects on this and that.

The Public Health Laboratory Service is a very kind organization to work for. It looks after you in the best sort of way and is flexible in allowing you to make career choices. If I pass my Part 2 exam I will probably finish my present job in about a year and then go abroad for a couple of years. At the moment pathology is a specialty with a need for more people, so I should be able to find a consultant post when I return.

Anaesthetics, radiology and radiotherapy

These specialties, which do not fit into the broad categories previously described, have certain features in common. They are all concerned with growing technological areas of medical practice, which means that job opportunities are good and research and teaching can play a large part in the work. They are also disciplines in which work patterns, to a large extent, can be predicted in advance and emergencies are few. Part-time posts are therefore possible and this is recognized by the provision of part-time training schemes. Many women doctors have been attracted to these posts because of this. There are more female consultants in these areas of medicine than in any other.

Anaesthetics. Anaesthetists have responsibility for a variety of methods of anaesthesia used for operations, and for pain control in such areas as obstetrics and intensive care. You can choose to work across a wide field acting in conjunction with surgeons and sometimes physicians, or you can specialize in one branch, in which case you are likely to have a more active involvement in the general management of patients.

Radiology. Radiology is concerned with the taking of X-rays. These can be required for diagnostic or investigative purposes and are taken on behalf of many hospital departments. The radiologist, therefore, provides a central information service and will be involved in consultations on a great variety of cases. The work can entail some highly technical procedures as well as the interpretation of X-ray photographs and, sometimes, clinical advice. The radiology department also forms a link between the hospital and local GPs who will often refer their patients there.

Radiotherapy. The radiotherapist works mainly with cancer patients to provide radiation treatment, and may also act as coordinator for other forms of treatment. Departments are usually based in a few large general hospitals because of the high cost of the equipment used for treatment. There is a high degree of patient involvement, as radiotherapists follow their patients throughout the course of their illnesses, accepting personal responsibility for them within the context of the whole medical team concerned with the case.

Obstetrics and gynaecology

Obstetrics is concerned with childbirth and the treatment of women before and after childbirth. It also encompasses family planning and contraception. Gynaecology is concerned with diseases and hygiene of women. In obstetrics, methods of treatment and attitudes to it have recently undergone considerable change. Technical advances have made detailed monitoring of pregnancy possible but, at the same time, some women have expressed the desire for more personal control over their treatment and a more natural approach. This apparent contradiction is, perhaps, slowly being resolved.

Postgraduate training for obstetrics and gynaecology is well defined. Unfortunately, because of the high incidence of emergency work, there are few part-time posts.

Becoming a consultant

The competitive and stressful aspects of the time spent in hospital training posts cannot be emphasized too greatly. You will constantly be contending for new posts. Normally, senior house officer posts are held for six months each, across a period of at least 18 months; registrar posts for one two-year period; senior registrar posts for three or more years. After this there is nowhere to go except to a consultancy, as training posts are not usually renewable. Each new post may mean moving to another area and this can cause much disruption, especially if you have a family.

Obviously, there is some wastage during the very long education process, so what happens to those people who opt out? In the past they often went into general practice but now, with far more stringent training requirements, this is not so easily achieved. Public health medicine also has its own training needs, and not everyone wants to work in this field. It is therefore sensible to decide sooner rather than later if you want to leave the hospital service, so that you feel able to devote the necessary time to alternative training. At present, the greatest wastage probably occurs at registrar level when most people will already have worked for up to two years following registration.

If you reach senior registrar level, the chances are that you will ultimately find a consultant post but if you have chosen a popular specialty you may find you have little choice about where you will be able to work. It is a good idea, both from the point of view of your own training and for your career prospects, to undertake a research project and/or a higher degree. This is often possible at senior registrar level. If you are able to offer this additional experience, you may well increase your chances in the consultancy stakes!

Salary scales

These are the standard scales from April 2000, the latest available; they are enhanced by additional payments for out-of-hours work and London weighting:

House officer	£17,260
Senior house officer	£21,535–28,760 (maximum after five years)
Registrar	£24,070–35,080 (maximum after four years)

Finding a job

Although it is worth making personal inquiries about posts in the specialty or geographical area that interests you, ultimately you will have to wait until a job becomes available. All posts are advertised in the *British Medical Journal*.

4 The doctor in the community

Introduction

For doctors who work in the community, people are of prime importance. General practitioners (GPs) are involved with individuals' problems, whether personal, social, organizational or environmental. They cannot see illness in isolation. Personal contact will be a major factor in their work. Over 33 per cent of GPs are women, many of whom work part-time.

General practice

More than half of all graduates in medicine enter general practice, and the GP has a unique position within the NHS. The local doctor's surgery is the only place except for some accident and emergency departments where patients present themselves as being, in their own estimation, in need of treatment. General practice is also the most personalized of all the health services, based close to patients' homes and with opportunities for long-term relationships between doctor and patient. Within this context, it is the doctor's job to give early treatment and continuing care for the great variety of problems and disorders presented by patients.

Primary care

Since the NHS was founded in 1948, there has been a widening of the scope of the discipline of general practice and primary care. Primary healthcare teams started up in the 1960s with the expectation that they would play a preventive role with regard to illness. GPs became not only reactive towards their patients but also proactive in that they identified and met individual patient needs. Services within the NHS provided at local level are currently (2000) being reorganized to ensure that patients do not see a GP when they really need a nurse; that they do not go to hospital when they need a GP; and that all patients receive good treatment. In future, GPs will take over much of the outpatient work at present performed by hospital doctors, such as monitoring diabetes or respiratory diseases and minor surgery, thus allowing hospital doctors to concentrate on complex surgery and acute illnesses. New primary care groups are being formed. They are groups of local healthcare and social care professionals who, together with patient and health authority representatives, take devolved responsibility for the healthcare needs of their local community. Each primary care group will comprise 20 to 30 group practices operating in the same area. In 1999 the first 481 primary care groups started to operate. In the long term, primary care groups will evolve into primary care trusts, the first of which were set up in April 2000. These are free-standing bodies accountable to the local health authority for commissioning care and for the provision of community services for their population, based on needs assessment.

Approximately 90 per cent of GPs work in group practices. This has many advantages – cooperation over working hours, increased accessibility outside surgery times, the ability to employ more ancillary staff and to offer a more comprehensive service, and the benefits of working alongside colleagues. A primary healthcare team that includes nurses, health visitors, counsellors, psychologists and sometimes social workers (care managers) staffs the group practices. This means that doctors can concentrate on the areas in which their expertise is really needed, knowing that they have all the necessary backup and that their work will not be done in isolation from the attendant social problems and preventive work.

Working conditions

General practitioners have to cope with many moral decisions. Although the underlying principle is that GP services are available for all, individual doctors are not obliged to accept patients on to their lists and can refuse those likely to prove difficult. The social consequences of this are obvious, and though most practices have a policy of accepting everyone in their area who asks to be registered, unfortunately there are those that do not.

General practice is challenging because of the variety and unpredictability of the work. With many patients, you will have no foreknowledge of their illness and you must constantly be refocusing on new problems. Most illnesses will be transitory or in their early stages, and you will be faced with the task of diagnosis on very little evidence. The illnesses themselves can cover everything imaginable.

Patients expect a certain degree of impersonality from hospital doctors, but they look for support and a personal relationship from their GP. However, they often find it difficult to explain the exact nature of their problems. A recent study of complaints against doctors showed that most were not related to clinical incompetence, rather to personal handling – a failure in communication. You have to be able to read between the lines when occasion demands. This is obviously the least definable, least teachable aspect of general practice, but it is also very important. Effective birth control provision for teenagers means, for example, that there has to be sympathy and understanding on the part of general practitioners who have to make sure that strict confidentiality is assured.

The great advantage of general practice is its stability. It is rooted in the local community and thrives on continuity. This means that most doctors tend to stay for long periods in the same practice, in contrast to hospital doctors who, at least during the training period, have to be constantly on the move.

Training

A three-year postgraduate training is statutory for all doctors wishing to become independent general practitioners. This combines hospital posts in relevant specialties with a year's experience as a registrar in general practice. The GP registrar year is a paid appointment under the supervision of an approved general practitioner trainer. Of the two years in hospital posts, at least six months have to be spent in each of two specialties from the following: accident and emergency medicine, general surgery, orthopaedic surgery, geriatric medicine, general medicine, paediatrics, obstetrics and gynaecology, and psychiatry. Those who wish to gain experience outside these fields should check with their local training adviser that what they propose is acceptable for accreditation.

During the registrar year, you will work in a practice under the supervision of one doctor who has been selected and briefed for the role. Initially you will spend some time sitting in on consultations, but usually you will soon find yourself working alongside the other doctors in the practice. Once you have completed your training you will be required to undergo a competency-based test known as summative assessment. One of the difficulties is that the qualities that make a good GP are not well suited to objective assessment. As things stand at present, the supervising doctor has to testify to the registrar's 'satisfactory completion' of the year but is given few definite criteria on which to make a judgement. It is not necessary to take any examinations, though many choose to do so. The relevant examination is the Membership of the Royal College of General Practitioners (MRCGP). This is regarded as the best assessment of the satisfactory completion of vocational training for general practice. The exam has no clinical component and consists of written and oral tests covering all branches of medicine, with an emphasis on problem-solving skills.

There are regional advisers in general practice throughout the UK who can provide information and advice about training schemes, including updating courses. A list of postgraduate training schools and contact points is provided in Chapter 9, pp 95–100.

Finding a job

The distribution of GPs throughout the country is controlled centrally to try to provide an even spread. There are some areas, notably London and the South East, which are considered to have their full quota of doctors and it is therefore possible to enter a practice only by filling an already established position. In other places, there is a shortage of doctors, and expansion of existing practices or applications to set up new ones will be welcomed.

Jobs are found in two ways. Group practices usually make their own appointments, either by invitation or advertising. Single-handed vacancies are advertised, and the appointments handled by the local health authorities that have the responsibility for all GP services in the area.

General practice is an area where it is particularly advisable to ensure that your outlook is similar to that of your colleagues. For this reason, whatever the difficulties or pressures of finding a job in an increasingly competitive field, it is necessary to be selective and settle only for a practice into which you feel you will fit. All doctors working in general practice within the NHS have to possess a certificate of prescribed or equivalent experience issued by the Joint Committee on Postgraduate Training for General Practice.

Jobs are also advertised in the *British Medical Journal*.

Remuneration

General practice differs from all other areas of medicine in that it is not salaried. The very complicated remuneration system is based on a number of factors. GPs are technically self-employed. The government sets an average amount that GPs are supposed to earn, known as the intended average net remuneration (IANR). Basic pay is based on the number of patients on a GP's list and the degree of deprivation of the area worked in. There is also a set of allowances and target payments. Expenses incurred by GPs in providing primary care to their patients are paid back to the profession in full. Some of these expenses are paid back to the GP by direct reimbursement and other expenses by indirect reimbursement.

A trainee. Trainee GPs earn 15 per cent above the salary of their previous post and receive additional allowances for car and travelling expenses etc. Typical starting salaries are around £18,000 (2000).

A principal. In group practices, the distribution of the practice income is a matter that is decided by the partners.

The average intended net income of a GP was set at £54,220 in April 2000. The actual amount GPs earn depends on the services they provide and expenses incurred. Those who work in modern, multiple-partner practices in urban areas can expect to earn at least £60,000, but a GP working alone in an inner city area is likely to earn only around £30,000 (2000).

Case Study

A general practitioner considers his registrar year

Mike *has finished his trainee year and now works in a health centre.*

When I decided to do medicine I didn't know any doctors. My main ideas came from television and it seemed attractive.

I don't know quite how medical schools select their students. I, in fact, did rather badly in my A levels but I was still offered a place. At my particular medical school we did a survey and found that 86 per cent of the students were from public schools and, of course, there were a lot of doctors' sons. I have no idea why I was accepted!

I wasn't terribly happy at medical school. I found it provided such an isolated form of education and I would have preferred to be at a university. Not a lot of questioning was encouraged. There was just a vast amount of learning, which took away your energy for any form of critical appraisal. I found psychiatry the most interesting subject, and for some time I thought that was what I wanted to do. I then began to see psychiatry as very separate from medicine. In psychiatry, I thought my medicine would not be used so I began to think about general practice. It is an area where you can develop your own interests, and this appealed to me.

I did my trainee year as a GP after two years in psychiatry, nearly a year on a paediatric ward, and various locums in areas such as old people's medicine and cancer therapy. Locum work is a good way of getting experience. My trainee year was rather a disappointment. I made a bad choice. I had just got married and chose the practice for the convenience of the area rather than for any other reason. I was also not very much in sympathy with my trainer.

Nevertheless, I learnt a lot just by doing the job. I went to the local Postgraduate Centre for a half-day a week and that was good. The course was slanted towards consultations – the doctor/patient relationship – and I found that helpful. For me, this is what matters most about general practice – being involved and getting to know people and their families over a period of time. It is the basis for everything you do, and is helpful in evaluating symptoms. I know that general practice is often thought of as second-rate medicine – you are not a specialist – but the GP does have a specialist contribution to make in terms of assessment of patients' needs and early diagnosis.

It can be quite exhausting emotionally. You come across many cancer patients, people with terminal illnesses; people die and you see bereaved people. And all the time you have the responsibility of recognizing illness at an early stage among a heavy workload.

The average consultation time is 8 to 10 minutes. You can feel quite alone; there is no structure, as in hospitals, to reduce the strain of the personal involvement. Also, being on call can be more of a strain than people realize. The phone might ring at any time, day or night. I go to a Balint group – eight doctors and a group leader – where we discuss difficult cases. Because the doctor/patient relationship is a personal one in general practice, the doctor gets involved too and you have to work out how to keep well yourself and not get worn out by it all. I find the discussions very helpful for this. Being in a health centre also helps. You are much less isolated and have the backup services of the whole health team. Altogether, I'm very biased in favour of general practice. I think it's a good job.

Public health medicine

Public health medicine is about preventing disease, prolonging life and promoting health. It is concerned with improving the health of the population rather than treating the diseases of individual patients. Each district health authority employs public health physicians whose job it is to monitor the health status of the community and identify health needs. They also develop programmes to reduce risk and screen for early disease, control communicable disease, foster policies that promote health and plan and evaluate the provision of health care.

Although public health physicians are medically qualified, the work they do is most akin to social administration, and the specialist training they must take reflects this. Public health doctors are employed throughout the NHS, in trusts, health authorities and boards, in government departments and in academic and research institutions.

Training

Before beginning specialist training, doctors are required to complete three years of clinical work in a variety of settings, concentrating on relevant aspects of long-term care such as geriatrics and so forth. After this, it is usually possible to be appointed to a two-year registrar post in public health medicine and embark on specialist study. The examination taken by public health physicians is the Membership of the Faculty of Public Health Medicine (MFPHM), and, like other postgraduate medical qualifications, it is taken in two parts. Unusually, though, it is taken after a course of formal teaching, the subjects taught being statistics, sociology, epidemiology, economics and management skills. The course is university based and can be taken in two ways: either full-time for one year, or as a sandwich course, involving a mixture of both theory and practice. Either way, you will remain in post and be paid your salary throughout. Part 1 of the MFPHM is taken by examination and Part 2 is awarded based on a research project. Like all other qualified doctors in the UK, public health physicians undertake Continuing Professional Development training to maintain and develop the knowledge, skills and attributes required for effective professional practice.

Working conditions

Public health physicians have no direct contact with patients. Their job is to respond to the requests of others – providing information on which decisions can be taken, carrying out research, seeing projects (such as the building of new health centres) through to their conclusion, and liaising with all sectors of the local health service. The public health physician is the main bridge between the doctors and the administrators. You will find yourself attending a lot of meetings, writing reports (which often need the approval of several committees before the recommendations you make can become effective) and generally finding out about the health needs, services and environmental conditions of your area. The amount of freedom you are allowed will vary from one authority to another, but in many places the job can be what you make it, and there will be opportunities to plan and carry out your own research projects.

The field is so wide that most people specialize within it and though everyone is employed in the general role of 'specialist in public health', most will hold responsibility for a particular aspect such as environmental health, social services liaison, information and planning, child health, prevention of disease etc.

If you are interested in the wider implications of medicine, a career in public health medicine is rewarding but you must be prepared to accept the pace at which results are achieved. Mostly this is very slow, as decision-making processes in bureaucratic institutions are extremely lengthy.

Public health physicians sit on district management teams and have a real role to play in the planning of services. There is a strong structure for multidisciplinary planning teams, which can be set up and run by community physicians. These present an opportunity for considering medical problems in a social context and making proposals accordingly. The job is varied and will bring you into contact with a great variety of people, including doctors, working in all sectors of the health service. It may well involve some undergraduate teaching and will have the advantages of a good salary and regular working hours.

Public health medicine is an expanding specialty, and prospects for employment are, overall, good.

Case Study

A public health physician discusses her work

Jenny *is the community physician for a socially mixed inner city area that has two teaching hospitals and a well-developed department of public health.*

I did an MSc course at the School of Hygiene in London, because I was interested in social aspects of disease and ways of bringing down the death rate. I also felt critical of the structure of the health service – the fact that it is so doctor-dominated. So I decided to come into public health.

I work as part of the area planning team, which consists of me, a nurse, a planning administrator, a finance officer and a works officer. There is virtually no contact with patients and often a very long-term feedback of achievements, which I think puts off quite a lot of younger people. On the other hand, the pay is good and you don't have the strain of the immediate responsibilities as you do in clinical work. If you make a mistake, the implications can be serious but you do not see the results of it under your nose!

A lot of the work is research and there are opportunities to follow your own inclinations here. Of course, not all the work goes in the directions you would like.

---

5   Dentistry

Introduction

In January 1998, there were 27,760 registered dentists in the UK, of whom 28 per cent were women. Around 21,000 dentists work in general practice, 2,500 in the Hospital Dental Service and 1,700 in the Dental Public Health Service. Eighty per cent of dental treatment is currently provided under the NHS. A few dentists are employed in the armed forces (see Chapter 6), university teaching and research, and large industrial companies. To practise in the UK, dentists have to register with the General Dental Council.

Much of a dentist's work is highly technical and requires a lot of manual dexterity. Today, with the emphasis on preventive work, the dentist is also expected to counsel and educate. People have to be persuaded to take proper care of their teeth and be shown how to do this. Anyone thinking of taking up dentistry must feel confident of his or her ability to combine both the technical and human aspects of the work.

Entrance requirements

All courses are run in conjunction with universities, and applications are made through the Universities and Colleges Admissions Service (contact points on p 85). You should consult *The UCAS Handbook* for the relevant year of entry: this will provide details of the admissions procedure and how to apply. Applications are normally made between 1 September and 15 December of the year preceding the year of entry. Prospective students are strongly advised to obtain prospectuses of the universities, schools and colleges in which they are interested before making their application, as courses and entrance requirements vary. There are 14 dental schools run in conjunction with universities in the UK and two in Ireland. Older people who have the Ordinary or Higher National Diploma but no GCSEs may find these qualifications are sympathetically considered by most schools.

Academic requirements for entrance to dental schools vary (see Chapter 9, pp 102–06 for details). All demand similar entrance qualifications, that is, three good A levels in chemistry, physics, maths, biology or zoology or, in Scotland, four or five Higher Grade SCEs. Many universities require a GCSE (or equivalent) pass in English language. If you are already a graduate you can bypass UCAS and apply direct to the particular college of your choice. Some institutions will waive entrance requirements in the case of mature students.

Dental colleges and contact points are listed in Chapter 9. A-level or other requirements and length of study are given after the addresses.

Training

Training for dentistry is demanding. Dental courses last for five years and lead to a bachelor's degree (either BDS or BChD). Some dental schools offer a pre-dental year for suitable candidates who lack relevant science subjects. The aim is to acquire an understanding of the scientific basis of dentistry, including the relevant medical sciences, scientific method and the evaluation of evidence. As a student, you will become aware of a wide range of problems that patients present and a variety of techniques that have been developed for their recognition, investigation, prevention and treatment.

The course consists of three main components that can be taught sequentially or concurrently in an integrated or modular arrangement. The first component consists of subjects common to medicine and dentistry, progressing from anatomy, physiology and biochemistry to the behavioural sciences (mainly psychology and sociology), epidemiology, law and ethics, pharmacology, pathology and microbiology to medicine and surgery. The second component includes instruction in subjects that comprise the oral and dental aspects of the biological sciences required for a detailed knowledge of the structure and function of the oral and dental tissues and of the related structures of the head and neck. The third component consists of the clinical and technical aspects of dentistry and prepares students for the provision of comprehensive oral and dental health care for patients of all ages. The oral and dental aspects of the biological sciences include theoretical and practical instruction in oral anatomy and physiology to provide a detailed knowledge of the form and structure of teeth. Students need to be fully aware of the importance of preventive methods, acquire diagnostic skills and understand the necessity of treatment planning before treatment procedures begin. The period of clinical studies will not be less than the equivalent of three and a third years of full-time study. Part of the dental curriculum has to be devoted to instruction in medicine and surgery. Students who wish to do so are encouraged to take an intercalated science degree, that is, an extra year studying basic medical sciences, usually between the second and third years of the dental course, to qualify for a BSc degree. Placements of students are encouraged for short periods in general dental practices where they can act as observers.

Funding

For the first four years of training, support for students on dental courses is on the same basis as for other higher education students. Students in year 5 and beyond will receive support from the Department of Health for the full cost of their tuition fees. They will also receive means-tested NHS bursaries for year 5 and beyond, towards the cost of their maintenance, and will be eligible for student loans for the balance of their maintenance costs during these years

General practice

Dentists who hold a contract under the NHS may provide a mixture of private and NHS treatment, both across their patient list and within the treatment they provide for one patient. A dentist does not have to accept all patients into NHS care but may choose to see some patients privately and others within the NHS. A patient who is currently registered for NHS care with a general dental practice is entitled to receive all the treatment needed under the NHS, but by arrangement with the dentist is entitled to choose to have some (or all) of his or her treatment privately.

There are two points that need to be considered carefully. All newly qualified people will benefit from the support and guidance of more experienced colleagues, and there are many advantages in working in a group practice. Hours can be more flexible, there are more resources available for specialist help, and it is easier to keep pace with developments when there are opportunities for discussion and the sharing of problems and ideas. In short, a group practice may be better both for the patient and the dentist.

Starting work in general practice

Newly qualified dentists are required to complete a year's vocational training before they can practise under an NHS contract. They work at the practice of an approved trainer for a salary. Most young dentists start working as associates in a group practice. Associates are self-employed dentists, responsible for the treatment provided but working in a practice owned by someone else. Later, they may become partners and ultimately set up on their own account. There are no set rules for this progression of responsibility. What individuals do will depend on the openings available and their own assessment of what is best; they can choose where they work and the hours they keep. Dentists in general practice also have the right to decide what work they will or will not carry out.

Working conditions

The aim of general practice is to get patients under continuous care – that is, to make them aware of the importance of regular treatment and to make them willing, whatever their fears or reservations, to return for that treatment. This can create a lot of pressure on the dentist, who must constantly be making two types of assessment: first, the clinical assessment of the work needing to be done; second, an assessment of the patient and the best manner in which to approach him or her. In any working day, this process is gone through many times, usually in the knowledge that a tight time schedule has to be kept.

The clinical work undertaken in general practice is wide. There are those who prefer to spend their days doing routine fillings, referring more difficult cases to hospital, but most dentists like the variety and satisfaction of offering a complete range of treatment. If you are going to work in this way, you need to be self-reliant, competent in all aspects of dental care, and able to work under pressure. As many people are apprehensive about dental treatment you must always appear confident and reassuring, however apprehensive you yourself may be feeling, and you will need a good deal of patience and tolerance when dealing with difficult people. You must also be able to work in cooperation with your surgery assistant and any specialist the practice may employ. With better dental hygiene and higher charges for NHS work, there has recently been more emphasis on preventive work and more complex dental treatment.

Case Study

A dental surgeon gives an account of group practice

Jane *works in a large practice in an inner city area.*

I trained at Kings in London. After qualifying, I spent six months working in a hospital as a house officer. It was a good way to start, because it helped me to build up my confidence within the support structure of the hospital. However, in all other ways I much prefer general practice. In hospital, as soon as you see something interesting you have to pass it on to the specialist, and usually you never find out what happens. I think teeth are specialized enough without specializing further within the field. In this practice, we never refer patients elsewhere. We do everything ourselves.

I enjoy the variety of work I get – everything from working with children to doing dentures for old people. I would hate to spend the day doing routine fillings endlessly. There are, of course, the difficult patients – usually the nervous ones who can be quite aggressive. I've often been asked, 'Are you sure you know what you're doing? You look a bit young.' Really, people like this are just asking for reassurance, and I look for a way of making them feel they are in control of the situation. I tell them to raise their left hand if anything hurts and that usually works. It *is* very hard work but I get a lot of job satisfaction from it. We are able to set our own working pace and I see about 16 patients a day. That's a low number but I feel that if I went much above that the quality of my work would suffer.

This is a large practice with five full-time and six part-time dentists, including people with special skills. With such a large staff we are able to give a very comprehensive service and to stay open well beyond normal hours. We never turn patients away. We have emergency hours when people can just walk in for treatment, and we find that our patients stay with us, even when they move away from the area. Probably this is because we are one of the few practices in this city to do bridges and crowns on the National Health Service. In fact, we do very little private work – only those things that the Health Service doesn't cover, mainly cosmetic work.

With so many dentists working together, we can have an instant second opinion and a fresh vision on any problems we may have.

Working in a hospital

Hospital work is salaried. Conditions of work are also similar to dentists working in general practice, except that there is more emphasis on outpatient clinics and long-stay patients are a rarity.

Treatment given to patients is usually more complex than that provided by general dental practitioners, and patients may have congenital abnormalities or facial injuries. Qualified dentists who wish to work in a hospital have to follow a similar path to that of hospital doctors, moving through the training grades and combining them with postgraduate study towards their chosen specialization. Hospital dentists generally work as part of a team.

Orthodontics

Orthodontics, at its simplest, is concerned with the straightening of crooked and misplaced teeth. This is done by means of specially made appliances. Undergraduate dental courses cover the basic aspects of orthodontics, and every dentist in general practice should know enough to tackle the simpler work.

There are, however, more complex forms of tooth misplacement, which involve far more than a mechanical correction. In these cases specialist knowledge of the development of the jaw is required, and the general practitioner may seek help by referring the patient to a hospital. The hospital staff work closely with local dentists, holding outpatient clinics where the patients referred by them can be seen. Much of the work will be advisory. The problem will be assessed and a report suggesting suitable treatment will be sent to the dentist. Often the work can then be carried out in the general practice surgery, and only extreme cases will be treated at the hospital.

Most district hospitals have a consultant orthodontist who has come to the post after eight or so years of postgraduate study. After qualifying, the first step to such a post is a job as a house officer, during which a postgraduate course in orthodontics can be taken. You then have to spend a number of years progressing through the training grades, until finally becoming eligible for a consultant post. The network of consultant orthodontists is small, however, and you may have to wait for a long time before a post falls vacant.

Orthodontists may also work in general practice, either establishing a surgery with this specialty or dividing their time between several practices in which they give their specialist help. Payment is on the same basis as other general practitioners.

Paediatric dentistry

Paediatric dentistry is concerned with understanding the normal growth and development, and promotion and maintenance, of oral health for children. Students should be responsible for the care of a number of children to assess their overall needs, the effectiveness of preventive measures, their behaviour, management and restorative treatment. Students also need to manage children who require emergency care, carry out diagnostic procedures, formulate treatment plans and relate them to comprehensive dental care for children. They should understand the special dental needs of children with disabilities and know about the management of developmental dental abnormalities.

Oral surgery

In oral and maxillofacial surgery, the dental and general surgical disciplines meet. It deals not only with the more difficult dental problems but also with accidental injuries to the facial region, facial cancer, abnormalities such as cleft palate, and deformities of the jaw. There are large areas of overlap with other medical specialties, and oral surgeons may work in conjunction with plastic surgeons and ear, nose and throat specialists, among others.

There are about 300 consultant oral surgeons in the UK, many of whom have taken both a dental and a medical training. It is possible to specialize in oral surgery without doing a medical training, but it involves spending longer in the training grades of hospital work and today there is an increasing preference for people with medical qualifications. Those who opt for this specialty have to undergo nine years of basic courses followed by a further eight years or so of postgraduate study and take the Fellowship in Dentistry, a difficult examination with a pass rate of only 10 to 15 per cent.

Case Study

A talk with a consultant oral surgeon

Most consultants work in district hospitals, dividing their time between one main and two subsidiary hospitals. They probably operate at least three times a week, are on call day and night with a colleague one week out of two, and run outpatient clinics at each of their hospitals. They are, perhaps, assisted by a senior house officer and a house officer, and have some responsibility for the further training of their younger staff.

Oral surgery is much the most fascinating and demanding aspect of dentistry. Although it overlaps with general surgery, it demands a practical knowledge of dentistry if the importance of many of the operations is to be understood. We operate on salivary glands, tumours, impacted wisdom teeth, deformed jaws and all kinds of facial injuries. The work is highly specialized and can lead to academic work and research for those who are interested.

Dental hygiene

A dental hygienist's role is to motivate patients to help keep their mouths healthy to avoid gum disease and tooth decay. A hygienist treats gum disease by scaling and polishing teeth to remove calculus and plaque, and applies fissure sealants and fluoride to children's teeth to reduce dental caries.

Two-year full-time courses to train as a dental hygienist are available at most dental schools. Study includes anatomy, physiology, preventive dentistry, oral health promotion and the management and care of patients. The minimum entrance requirements are five GCSEs and two 'A' levels.

Most dental hygienists work in one or more dental practices within the NHS and privately. There is a growing need for dental hygienists to work with patients who have special needs, either in the dental surgery on in the patient's home. In the community, dental hygienists may work with children, people with special needs and older people in residential care.

Dental public health

The Service is concerned with public health matters as well as treatment, and fulfils an educational role, running projects, mounting exhibitions and visiting schools, day centres, old people's homes etc. Much of the treatment is carried out in local clinics but there are regular school inspections as well as project-based work that take staff out of the clinics and provide a stimulating variety to their working life.

All posts in dental public health are salaried, so the service represents an attractive alternative for people who do not want to work within the direct payment system of general practice. It would also satisfy those who want to work in a wider community context and who want a defined career structure. Newly qualified dentists can apply for jobs as dental public health officers and, while they are in this post, have the option of taking a postgraduate course in Dental Public Health. The following grade in the career structure is assistant district dental officer, who is usually involved in a specialist area and who will have the opportunity for research. Then there is the district dental officer and finally the post of consultant in dental public health, which carries considerable responsibility for the organization and general policy of the service.

Case Study

A dental public health officer talks about her job

Linda's *position is not typical, as her job is a joint appointment between the Community Dental Service and a local teaching hospital. It does, however, give some interesting indications of the future directions community dentistry may take.*

After qualifying, two and a half years ago, I didn't want to work under the financial pressures of general practice and I definitely wanted a salaried job. I felt that hospital work was too inward looking, so the community service seemed to answer my needs.

I wanted to work with the elderly and, fortunately, I had this opportunity when a special project was set up to treat handicapped adults. Many elderly people come into this category. I now have an interesting combination of clinical work, hospital work, home visits and research, which I find very satisfying. At the clinic, I treat children and handicapped adults; at the hospital, I deal with elderly patients who need dentures; on my home visits I do work for housebound people. I have one day a week set aside for my research. I'm researching the dental needs of elderly people in residential homes and geriatric hospitals, and my findings will be presented for an MPhil or a PhD.

I think that the image of the community service is beginning to change. It used to be thought of as the unpopular branch of dentistry, which treated those people in whom no one else was interested. So it used to get the dregs – people passing through for experience or dentists who saw it as an easy option. Now, with more backup from the health authorities and with an expanded role, it is seen as a career. There is bound to be more emphasis on the handicapped in the future, so there will be a lot of new ground to be broken and the opportunities for research and planning are exciting.

Occupational and industrial practice

A number of large companies have, for many years, provided dental treatment facilities for staff at work and a significant proportion of the adult working population is currently served in this way. Although dental services are better known among the larger organizations, there have been instances where groups of smaller companies have joined locally to share the advantages of a common dental practice. The company usually provides the premises and equipment and pays the dental staff. Treatment is generally provided under the NHS with staff paying the statutory contribution and the fees being assigned by the practitioner to the company.

Career opportunities within occupational dentistry are limited because of the relatively small number of posts available. Posts in occupational and industrial dentistry are advertised in the professional journals; generally a company would expect a successful applicant to have had appropriate experience in general practice, although a broader experience may be an advantage.

Case Study

A senior dental officer discusses occupational dental practice

Bill *coordinates the dental services that are available to staff working in the head office of a large retail organization.*

I have worked in occupational dentistry for several years, having worked previously in hospital and general practice. In the practice where I work there are approximately 4,500 employees and comprehensive dental care is provided for the benefit of staff. The practice comprises three full-time dentists, one part-time dentist, one full-time oral hygienist, two part-time oral hygienists, five dental nurses, one receptionist, one secretary and one clerical assistant. There are five well-equipped surgeries with a panoramic X-ray machine and an oral hygiene area where patients can be given instruction on a one-to-one basis. Approximately 70 per cent of staff regularly use the facilities provided. There is complete clinical freedom, and the majority of the treatment is carried out under the NHS with staff paying the statutory contribution.

Our dental practice is part of an occupational health department with other health professionals. It includes doctors, occupational nurses, physiotherapists, chiropodists and an osteopath, and so for me there is the added enjoyment of being part of a team fulfilling a vital role which is valued by the company it serves.

Updating

A new scheme launched in April 2000 and to be implemented in October 2000 requires dentists to update their training. Over a five-year period, 250 hours of continuing professional development will be required to help dentists keep pace with developments in the field. Further information can be obtained from the General Dental Council (see p 102) or postgraduate dental schools listed on pp 106–09 in Chapter 9.

Remuneration

Within the NHS, adults now pay dentists under a fee per item basis; that is, the dentist receives a set fee for each procedure carried out. As far as children are concerned, a mixture of fees pays dentists for each item of treatment and monthly payments for each child on their list. Outside the NHS, each dentist sets private fees individually.

From their earnings, dentists have to equip and maintain their surgery and pay any staff they employ, for example receptionists or surgery assistants. Being in general practice is therefore rather like running a small business, with all the administrative problems but also with all the advantages of independence.

General practice. In general practice, a dentist working for the NHS only is likely to earn an average wage of £46,700 per annum, while a dentist providing both NHS and private treatment can expect to earn an average of a little over £55,000 (1997–98 figures).

Community dentistry. Income ranges from £23,410 to £54,740 (1997–98 figures).

Hospital service. Dentists are paid according to their hospital grade; salaries range from £16,710 for house officers to £61,605 for consultants (1997–98 figures).

Finding a job

The main source of job advertisements is the *British Dental Journal*, published every fortnight and free to BDA members. Apart from this, dental schools occasionally post job advertisements on their notice boards. If you are interested in working in community dentistry it is worth making a direct inquiry to the district dental officer of the area where you would like to work, as there may be unfilled posts not currently being advertised. House officer posts are usually obtained through the member of staff at your dental school who deals with arrangements for postgraduate training.

6 Working for the Armed Services and working abroad

The Armed Services

The Armed Services offer doctors and dentists relevant experience for eventual civilian work, either through a short service commission or a permanent career with good pay and prospects and pension. Self-contained living communities for Service personnel and their families are provided, together with their own medical facilities. There are opportunities for doctors and dentists, both male and female, to serve either in general practice or in a hospital setting. The scope of the work is similar to that within the NHS, as most of it entails caring for the health needs of servicemen and women and their families. In addition, however, there is the work generated by the activities of the Services themselves – occupational health, aviation medicine, underwater medicine and exercises in medical practice in war conditions.

Medical and dental officers live in the community into which they are posted, which may be abroad or, in the case of the Navy, on board a ship. All facilities, including housing, recreational and sporting amenities, are provided. You will be an officer of the Service first, wear the appropriate uniform, and be subject to the usual discipline; you will be a doctor or dentist second, but you will be clinically independent and your professional judgement will be trusted. Although there is usually a will to meet your wishes in the matter of postings, this does not always happen and, at the end of the day, you will go where you are sent. You will be obliged to serve the length of your commission.

Training

All applicants must receive their undergraduate training in the normal way at a medical or dental school before they begin work with any of the Services. There are financial advantages, however, in deciding to enter one of the Services during your student years by applying for a Ministry of Defence (MOD) cadetship.

Student cadetships

Each Service operates an identical medical sponsorship scheme (Cadetships) for the last three years before graduation. Acceptance is subject to a successful appearance before a selection board. You are commissioned Second Lieutenant (or equivalent ranks in the RN and RAF), your fees are paid for by the MOD and you will receive a salary. As part of the contract, you have to spend a set period after full registration on a six-year short service commission working for the Service concerned. There is little or no commitment to the military during your three-year undergraduate training.

Induction courses

Each Service has its own short induction course for entrants. This covers three main areas: general service training, which includes basic exercises; some practise of medical procedures in simulated war conditions; a study of your specialist subject as it relates to the activities of the Service.

Postgraduate training

All the Services have their own hierarchy of medical and dental responsibility, and internal training sessions are arranged for recent entrants. In addition, there are opportunities for post-graduate training which fulfil the requirements of the various Royal Colleges. All Services offer vocational training in general practice and a number of hospital specialties. There is a general emphasis on occupational medicine, and training facilities are good. In most cases, training undertaken during a short commission will be a recommendation for subsequent civilian work.

The Royal Army Medical Services is divided into two main divisions: The Royal Army Medical Corps (RAMC) and The Royal Army Dental Corps (RADC). There are opportunities for GMC-registered doctors to serve a short service commission with the RAMC. Postgraduate medical training for army doctors include the following specialties: accident and emergency medicine, anaesthetics and resuscitation, burns and plastic surgery, general medicine, general surgery, ophthalmology, orthopaedic surgery, psychiatry, radiology and public health medicine. Contact the Royal Army Medical Corps in Aldershot, Hampshire for further information (see p 109).

The Royal Navy Medical Service (RNMS) employs medical officers on a short career commission basis of six years. Specialist training starts after about three years in all major disciplines except obstetrics, gynaecology and paediatrics. For further information contact the Royal Navy Medical Service in Hampshire (see p 109).

The Royal Air Force (RAF) employs General Duties Medical Officers (GDMOs) who spend about 18 months working in vocational hospital-based training posts followed by another 18 months working in a medical centre on an RAF base which is approved for GP vocational training. Specialists are also employed. Postgraduate training in your chosen specialty is provided as well as training in aviation medicine. For further information, contact the RAF in Sleaford, Lincolnshire (see p 109).

Case Study

A junior medical officer talks about her first RAF posting

Pat *was introduced to the crew of the Search and Rescue squadron and to her new role quickly.*

On the most recent trip, I was just about to go down to the married quarters to check on a family when they called me over the storno [radio communication] and said, 'Turn round, come back. They need you.'

At that point they'd been told there was someone who'd had his legs severed in an accident on a ship, so we had to leave extra quickly because he'd be losing vast amounts of blood if this really was the case. I just took my kit in my bag, jumped in the back of the helicopter and got changed inside.

When we got there, it was the middle of the night and the men were deep down in the hold of the ship. They put the winchman down first and then me. The boat was really throwing around, but we found this pitch-black hole that stank of petrol and diesel, and we got down and found that there were two people involved. One was dead, or presumed dead, and the other was injured. I couldn't actually stand up because the boat was throwing itself around so much that I'd just have been thrown against the side of the ship. So I had to kneel down, and even then I was sliding everywhere.

I discovered (working by torchlight) that his leg wasn't severed; it was badly broken, a compound fracture, and someone had put a belt across so he hadn't lost a desperate amount of blood. I gave him some analgesia, strapped him into the stretcher and the winchman started getting him up to the top of the ship.

I did feel ill when I was down there, but you just have to get on with it.

Working abroad

If you would like to spend some time working abroad, there are opportunities for doctors and, to a lesser extent, dentists to do much-needed work in developing countries and countries in Eastern Europe. Workers are needed for both short- and long-term commitments, but the average time spent in such posts is around two years.

If travel is your main objective, you will probably be disappointed. Many jobs are in remote rural areas, and the demands of the work will leave you with little time to travel far except during your annual leave. The rewards are of a different kind, in terms of the experience you will gain. Your knowledge and training will be a rare commodity and you are likely to find yourself taking on considerable responsibility at a much earlier stage than you would in the UK. Flexibility and resourcefulness will be called for, as you will be working, much of the time, without sophisticated equipment and with an erratic supply of drugs. Many Third World countries are in the process of establishing a health service – often, and probably inappropriately, modelling it on the Western pattern. This can mean that almost the entire health budget is spent on one prestige teaching hospital in the capital city, which will be inaccessible to the majority of the population. However, there are interesting projects being set up to provide primary care for rural areas and to explore the most effective ways of improving health. As most illness in developing countries arises from poverty, malnutrition and poor sanitation, education is an important part of medical care. Many projects are community based and doctors will be involved in the training of auxiliary workers who return to their own communities to work. This is challenging work and should be a two-way process, with the doctors learning from the communities they serve what their needs and problems are and how best they can be met.

Finding work

There are three main types of organization through which work can be found. These are government agencies, volunteer organizations such as Voluntary Service Overseas, and missionary societies. Each offers somewhat different conditions of work and, practical considerations apart, will appeal to people in sympathy with their particular ethos.

GOVERNMENT AGENCIES

The Department for International Development is responsible for Britain's overseas aid to developing countries, for global environmental assistance and for assistance to Eastern Europe and the former Soviet Union. The organization recruits staff for projects funded under British aid. All posts are held on contracts.

In developing countries, posts are focused in the following key areas: health sector planning management and financing; population programmes; sexually transmitted diseases, including HIV and AIDS, and communicable disease control. There is a need for health economists, health programme and field managers, health building managers (for hospitals), health planners, health project directors, hospital managers and population experts.

Applicants should have considerable experience in developing countries and, as far as possible, training, management and policy development skills. Contact the Department for International Development (p 110) for further information.

VOLUNTEER ORGANIZATIONS
Voluntary Service Overseas (VSO)
This organization runs an extensive volunteer programme of which a small part (about 15 per cent) is in the health field.

The projects they sponsor are chosen carefully to fit in with the need for a fairer distribution of services. This means concentrating on local health care which does not rely on expensive technology, and doctors in technological specialties are rarely accepted. The emphasis is on a community approach, and a critical attitude towards the organization of services is encouraged.

Working conditions
VSO workers are volunteers who are expected to stay for a minimum of two years with their project and are responsible to their immediate employers. They are paid a living allowance at the same rate as their colleagues in the local community and are provided with accommodation. VSO will pay National Insurance, fares, medical cover, insurance, professional fees and small equipment grants. The organization also contributes to endowment schemes and will post couples where both have relevant skills. Most volunteers live as part of the local community, as their work will be less effective if they are seen as outsiders. This means that knowledge of the local language is vital, and VSO organizes preparation courses in England to help with this.

Qualifications required
Doctors should have at least three years' post-registration experience, preferably in obstetrics, paediatrics, accident and

emergency, general medicine, tropical diseases or general practice. Dentists should have two years' post-qualifying experience. Contact VSO for further information.

International Health Exchange (IHE)

The organization provides appropriately trained personnel for organizations that run programmes in countries in Africa, Asia, the Pacific and Eastern Europe. It also links health professionals and the organizations working for health improvement in developing countries. In addition, the IHE also works to provide greater understanding among health professionals of the health and human resource needs of developing countries and is specifically working to encourage recognition by the UK NHS of the mutual benefits of working in developing countries.

The International Health Exchange runs an international register of health workers as well as short training courses and workshops. Contact the IHE for further information.

MISSIONARY SOCIETIES

Missionary societies have been traditionally involved in medical work, and for a long time local mission hospitals provided the only medical care available to large sections of the population in developing countries. Most of the work is still hospital based, usually in quite small units, but there is an increasing tendency towards the establishment of primary healthcare clinics and the employment of local workers.

Working conditions

To work for a missionary society you need to be a practising Christian. Missionaries tend to generate a feeling of community and shared faith, which can make overseas work a rewarding way of life for believing Christians. Jobs are available on a long- and short-term basis, some in well-established settings and some out in the field, developing new services or responding to crises.

Finding a job

The Medical Missionary Association acts as a clearinghouse for all posts available through the UK missionary societies. They publish a magazine, *Saving Health*, which carries a list of health professionals needed overseas in mission settings. Medical Missionary Association staff are available to give individual advice and information about opportunities for work abroad with mission organizations. Each year in May they hold a seminar for medical students planning to spend their 'elective' abroad.

Christians Abroad is an ecumenical agency of the Council of Churches for Britain and Ireland. It provides information and advice about opportunities for voluntary or paid work in aid, development and mission overseas. There is an information base for agencies seeking professional development or relief workers. The organization provides a consultancy for overseas recruitment and personnel management to agencies placing persons overseas in mission and development.

Christian Vocations produces two publications that contain medical opportunities. *Jobs Abroad*, published twice a year, comprises over 3,000 vacancies outside the UK of interest to Christians. The *Short Term Service Directory* focuses on positions of up to two to three years' duration and is published annually.

The Medical Service Ministries provides funding for medical missionaries overseas.

For further information about working abroad, see pp 110–11 for contact points.

Alternative medicine

Introduction

Alternative medicine is rapidly becoming accepted in the UK, and the past 10 years have seen a very substantial increase in the number of practitioners in the field. It is no longer regarded with suspicion or as something cranky. Roughly one-third of the total adult population in the UK use an alternative therapy at least once a year and currently (2000) there are over four million visits a year to alternative practitioners. Most therapies are based on sound principles. If they were more widely accepted, more people might enjoy better health without recourse to drug or surgical treatment. Many people think that within 10 years a number of alternative therapies will be accepted as part of conventional medicine and already there are increasing numbers of practitioners operating within the NHS. At the moment, the only therapy currently widely available under the NHS is homoeopathy. Other therapies that have recently become more available include acupuncture and aromatherapy. Usually, however, practitioners operate a private service and charge their patients fees.

It should be noted that training is very rarely funded so students should expect to finance their own training.

Holistic medicine

Alternative therapies accept that treatment has to be given holistically, taking the mind, body and spirit of an individual into account. Consideration of the whole person is regarded as essential. Illness, or disease, is seen as an imbalance or disharmony within the mind, body, spirit, or as the result of an accumulation of harmful substances. The latter can usually be traced back to an individual's lifestyle, such as unsuitable diet, bad posture, lack of exercise, or build-up of stress. Great emphasis, therefore, is placed on living well, having a healthy diet with lots of exercise and plenty of rest. It is believed that the body has the power to heal itself, so the job of the therapist is to diagnose and then remove obstructions to the self-healing process. This is done through various, often very different, forms of therapy. Many therapies in use today derive from ancient medical systems, often from the East. Others, of more recent origin (mostly emanating from the USA), make use of high technology to measure the body's responses. Some practitioners use several therapies to treat a problem rather than one only.

Qualities required of practitioners

You have to be in sympathy with the philosophy of the therapy you wish to study, and some therapies require a rigorous study of science subjects such as physiology, anatomy and biology. Knowledge of these is necessary, as you may have to be able to make a medical diagnosis of patients to determine whether a particular form of therapy is appropriate. Furthermore, you must have the 'feel' and manual skills for the therapies you wish to practise. You also have to have an empathy with people and a real desire to help them.

Organization of training and practice

It can be hard finding one's way around the field. The fact that there are often no controls on either who can set up in practice, or what constitutes training for the given therapy, presents difficulties both for would-be practitioners and for patients. To counteract this, many alternative therapies already have, or are in the process of setting up, their own professional associations to ensure high standards of training and treatment. Only approved professional bodies are listed in this book. Students who successfully complete a training course at a ratified institution are accepted as members of the relevant professional institution and are entitled to use its letters of qualification after their names. They are also included in the society's list of qualified practitioners and, in return, have to accept the ethical code of practice imposed by the institution.

It is not advisable to enter alternative medicine by any route other than recommended training establishments. It is vital to undergo a thorough training at an approved college. Practitioners should do everything possible to ensure a high standard of professionalism in the service they provide.

Some of the very many alternative therapies available are very briefly described below. For further details contact a new (2000) Web site, www.healingonline.co.uk, geared towards health professionals and working with all alternative practitioner organizations, that provides information about therapies and in-depth articles and research that inform professional development.

Details of training institutions can be obtained from the professional associations provided at the end of the explanation of the therapies given below. Their contact points are given in Chapter 9 pp 112–15.

Acupressure

Acupressure is a form of massage that is used in China for treating common ailments and for boosting the body's immune system. It is part of Traditional Chinese Medicine. Over the past 10 years it has become very popular in the UK and to a limited extent is now available under the NHS. It is used to treat many problems such as dizziness, fatigue, headaches, indigestion, insomnia, nausea, sinusitis, vertigo and vomiting. Studies have shown that acupressure helps to relieve nausea caused by anaesthesia and induced by pregnancy. Fingers, thumbs, feet and knee pressure are used to massage certain parts of the body.

Practising acupressure

There are very few therapists in the UK who practise acupressure only. Almost all practise acupuncture (see below). For details about training, contact the British Acupuncture Council.

Acupuncture

This is a therapy derived from China and is part of Traditional Chinese Medicine. Conditions that can successfully be treated include migraine, headaches, ulcers and digestive troubles, rheumatic conditions, eczema and other skin ailments, high blood pressure, depression and anxiety states, asthma and bronchitis. Acupuncture can also be used to induce anaesthesia and to treat various forms of addiction.

The therapy is based on the Chinese belief in the flow of energy, known as Qi, which needs to be kept in a state of equilibrium in the body. The energy flows along 14 main circuits known as meridians. Equilibrium is maintained by dispelling surplus energy at certain points on the meridians and by shifting energy to deficient areas. Illness is indicative of a loss of equilibrium, and the acupuncturist's job is to restore the balance by piercing the skin at appropriate points (known as acupoints) on the body. This involves diagnostic skill and a knowledge of the meridians and the acupoints at which the skin can be pierced.

Practising acupuncture

Many registered doctors practise acupuncture in addition to their normal medical work and opportunities for treating patients under the NHS are beginning to emerge. Some hospitals offer acupuncture for pain relief, particularly for ante- and post-natal treatments and in rheumatology units.

If you are not a doctor but are a practising acupuncturist, you are most likely to work in the private sector, alone, in a group practice, or in a health clinic. Through membership of a professional association, you can obtain insurance at advantageous rates. To train, you may be able to obtain a career development loan or perhaps (though unlikely) a grant from your local authority.

The British Acupuncture Council acts as a negotiating body for all legal and political matters that affect the practice of acupuncture and coordinates codes of practice, ethical procedures and standards for acupuncture in the UK. From 2002, all training courses will last three years full-time. Middlesex University provides a five-year degree in Traditional Chinese Medicine, of which acupuncture is a part, and the University of Westminster offers a three-year degree in acupuncture.

Case Study

An acupuncturist outlines his career

Richard is a registered doctor who now practises and teaches acupuncture.

Because of family pressures to choose a career with financial security, and my own interest in animals, I decided to become a vet. I did my first two years of pre-clinical studies and it was very interesting. I became very good at table football and learnt a bit about veterinary work as well! Then I did an intercalated year for a BSc in neurophysiology, and became very interested in behaviour and pain. After this, the veterinary clinical course was a terrible letdown. It was so turgid, tedious and dogmatic that I decided not to complete it. I decided to switch to medicine. I had to work for a year to get some money together because I had lost some of my grant in the process of changing courses, but this time I carried on to the end.

Sometime while I was a student, acupuncture hit the scene. I remember it well, as it was one of the major breakthroughs of my life. There was an article in a Sunday paper about an American in Beijing who had anaesthesia through acupuncture for an appendix operation. He was astonished! I thought: 'Here is someone who is objective and he believes in it.' Shortly after this, an acupuncturist visited a patient of mine and talked about his work, and I became more interested. Eventually, I combined acupuncture with the final year of my medicine course. I qualified in acupuncture shortly before qualifying in medicine.

I had a lucky break. I met an acupuncturist who needed some assistance and later I took over his practice for a year while he was on a sabbatical. He is involved with a radical NHS general practice, which operates as a collective and offers acupuncture treatment. I became involved too, and I've worked at the practice for three years now, partly as a doctor and partly as an acupuncturist.

I also do teaching on an acupuncture course. I teach the first medical year and I also teach in the college clinic. This is one of the 'quack' courses, and my association with it makes me unacceptable to the medical acupuncturists. It's all nonsense really. There's not as much difference between the two camps as people normally think. Within orthodox medicine there are so many disciplines and viewpoints, yet they co-exist. In acupuncture it is a parallel situation. The underlying concept is energy – it's a substance. You can consider it from this fundamental view, or be pragmatic. Or you have a third choice. You can be scientific and think one day you will find the nerve patterns to prove it all. In practice, what happens is similar to what happens in orthodox medicine. You try the simple solution first, and if that doesn't work you delve deeper, until eventually you are working with energy patterns, with individuality, and the total person.

Alexander Technique

The Alexander Technique is named after Frederick Matthias Alexander. An actor living at the beginning of the twentieth century, he had problems with his voice. He developed new body postures that not only rid him of the problems but also gave him a feeling of well-being.

The self-help technique aims to teach people to move freely and to discard the restricted movements and unnatural postures of bodily misuse they have adopted over the years. Practitioners prefer to call themselves teachers of pupils (students are trainee teachers) rather than label themselves as doctors who treat patients. The Alexander Technique is primarily used for enhancing physical and psychological good health and well-being rather than for directly healing physical and mental problems, but nevertheless has been found to relieve many chronic and even acute conditions such as backache, asthma, hypertension, irritable bowel syndrome and repetitive strain injury.

Practising the Alexander Technique

Teachers usually work on a one-to-one basis with sessions lasting around three-quarters of an hour. Training is very comprehensive and lengthy, lasting a minimum of three years full-time. For further details, contact the Society of Teachers of the Alexander Technique.

Aromatherapy

Aromatherapy is the fastest-growing alternative therapy in the UK and both doctors and nurses are becoming increasingly aware of its benefits. In December 1998 a survey conducted by South Bank University found that aromatherapy was the most popular alternative therapy used in both NHS and private hospitals.

Essential oils, extracted from plants, possess therapeutic properties. They are absorbed through the skin in various ways, for example, massage, inhalation and compresses, to alleviate many symptoms of illness and to promote well-being and good health. Aromatherapy is known to alleviate a great many problems and treatment is excellent when used to alleviate the anxiety, pain and stress suffered by cancer patients and patients who are suffering pre- or post-operative stress. It can also reduce the side effects of chemotherapy, which is why treatment is offered in many hospitals and hospices, as well as in some special schools and prisons. In addition, aromatherapy has proved remarkably effective in treating arthritis and rheumatism. Increasingly, GPs are allowing aromatherapists to practise in their surgeries.

Practising aromatherapy

Unfortunately, lack of approved training means there are problems for practitioners who want aromatherapy to be seriously considered. Statutory regulations are currently (2000) being considered and since June 1998 national occupational standards have been set up in agreement with the UK government and all reputable aromatherapists. It is essential to receive proper training in order to practise as an aromatherapist. Contact the Aromatherapy Organizations Council (AOC) for information about reputable training organizations. The AOC and Middlesex University have agreed a joint programme for a phased development leading to a full BSc degree in aromatherapy. Interim awards are currently being put in place at university diploma and advanced diploma levels.

Chiropractic

Chiropractors treat disorders of the spine, joints and muscles by manual adjustment, often with the help of X-rays. The focus is on the spinal vertebrae but they also work on the muscles, ligaments, joints, bones and tendons, aiming to improve function, relieve pain and increase mobility. The manipulative process may have a positive effect on the nervous systems and can relieve conditions such as asthma and irritable bowel syndrome that are not musculo-skeletal. Drugs and surgery are never used because chiropractors claim that when body systems are in harmony the body can heal itself.

Practising chiropractic

Medical practitioners are increasingly referring patients to chiropractors on the NHS. The profession has recently become regulated and all practitioners have to undergo a rigorous training that lasts for at least three years full-time. Contact the General Chiropractic Council for further details. The University of Glamorgan provides a four-year degree course in chiropractic and the University of Westminster a three-year degree course.

Flower remedies

Dr Edward Bach created flower remedies in England during the early part of the twentieth century. He had an intuitive knowledge of plants and made in-depth studies of personality types. He claimed that flower remedies harmonized the imbalances of the psyche and that physical problems manifested as a result of dis-ease, a conflict of the emotions. Contact the Dr Edward Bach Foundation for details of training in Bach flower remedies.

Healing

Healing has been practised for thousands of years, and there are far more healers in the UK than anywhere else in the world. It is not a therapeutic system but is based on the belief in a higher reality that orders our physical world with which we must be in harmony. A breakdown of harmony causes illness. Healers create a bond of empathy between themselves and their patients and allow their mind energies to flow into their patients and restore them to harmony with the higher reality.

Practising healing

Contact either the Confederation of Healing Organizations or the National Federation of Spiritual Healers for details of how to train as a healer.

Case Study

A healer talks about her powers

Elizabeth *became aware of her healing powers at an early age, and for years sought the path of healing she should follow. Eventually she perfected a preparation of flower potencies, which is used worldwide with great success.*

I was a powerful healer by the age of four. At the beginning I practised on animals, and my first notable healing was of a puppy I adored. One night, as I was going to bed, I saw it in terrible distress through poisoning. I ran to it and automatically did what is called 'combing the aura'. By making 'combing' motions around my puppy I saved his life. It is a question of empathy – you feel terribly sorry for the suffering animal or person and this is what brings out your healing ability.

At the age of 17 I started to train as a nurse at St Thomas's. But, very early on, I discovered vivisection and I was so horrified that eventually I couldn't finish the course. That made me turn my back on conventional medicine. Instead, I studied alternative therapies – some in considerable depth. None matched up to what I was looking for. When I was 44 I got direct clear intelligence which, over the course of years, led me to the method by which the energies given off by flowers can be radically modified and stored in simple preparations – which then act as batteries containing the energy.

My preparations are unique. Drugs work on the physical body and homoeopathic medicines on the psychic body (that is, on radiations or emanations from the physical body). My flower potencies do neither. What they do is to remove the psychological and emotional blocks stopping a being from accepting the gifts that God continually gives. A by-product of these gifts is health.

The energy in the preparations cannot be analyzed chemically but can be measured on a voltmeter and it is the energy that is the active principle that does the healing. Because the preparations have no bad side effects they are a simple, safe self-therapy. They can remove any infective or diseased condition and have proved effective in cases of the most severe injury, and of terminal cancer. They ease and smooth the path of the dying. I have never known them to fail if correctly used.

Herbal medicine (Western)

Western herbal medicine as practised today in the UK is the accumulation of many centuries of wisdom. Many plants are used – in some instances the flowers, stems and roots – as well as parts of trees and seaweed. They are used both to heal and to ensure continued good health. Trained medical herbalists prescribe plant-based remedies in the form of lotions, ointments, poultices, syrups, essential oils and tablets. In the case of illness, these are intended to restore the body's equilibrium and help it to heal itself. Medical herbalists question their patients at length about their medical and family histories, allergies, and reactions to drugs, diet and general lifestyles. They will then prescribe medicines according to individual needs and not solely based on specific illnesses. The medicinal herbs may eliminate unwanted substances from the body, for detoxification or for promoting good health in an already healthy body. Remedies have been found to be instrumental in alleviating many problems, including arthritis, cystitis, depression, digestive problems, migraines, nausea, oedema, psoriasis, stress–related conditions, thrush and vaginitis.

Practising herbal medicine

Contact the National Institute of Medical Herbalists for accredited training in medical herbalism. Middlesex University provides a three-year degree course in herbal medicine and the University of Central Lancashire a four-year degree course.

Homoeopathy

Homoeopathy is practised either by a number of medical doctors who have undertaken specialist training in homoeopathy and who may be working for the NHS, or professional homoeopaths who are qualified only in this field. The former may use a combination of homoeopathic and mainstream medical practices, while the latter will use only homoeopathic remedies. Homoeopathy is a treatment of the whole person, and symptoms are seen as 'expressions of disharmony within the whole person'. When homoeopathic doctors and homoeopaths take a case history, they pay attention not only to the patient's description of the symptoms but also to his or her personality, likes and dislikes. Because they realize that individuals react to illness in different ways, they will not always give the same treatment for the same illness. Disease is treated by the use of very small amounts of a substance, a minimal dose that, in healthy persons, produces symptoms similar to those of the condition being treated. Remedies are produced from plant, mineral and animal sources and may be in the form of pills, powders, granules or tinctures and, because they are administered in minute doses, they produce no side effects. Remedies can be used to alleviate almost any reversible illness in adults, children or animals. The healing process is gentle and designed to activate the body's own restorative powers.

Practising homoeopathy

If you want to train as a homoeopath and are already medically qualified you can take a six-month course under the jurisdiction of the Faculty of Homoeopathy and subsequently practise in one of the homoeopathic NHS hospitals. If, however, you are not medically qualified but wish to become a homoeopath you can undertake a rigorous four-year course under the auspices of the Society of Homoeopaths. The University of Central Lancashire provides a four-year degree course in homoeopathic medicine.

Hypnotherapy

Hypnotherapy uses hypnosis to tap into the unconscious to achieve behavioural change. Hypnosis is a state of altered consciousness during which the unconscious mind becomes receptive to suggestion. To observers, people under hypnosis appear to be sleeping, but they are awake and aware of what is happening. The awareness experienced, however, is different from that experienced in an ordinary conscious state, with the reality of the external world being relegated to the back of their minds while they experience increased receptivity and responsiveness to suggestions received from therapists. Hypnotherapy has had many successes in the treatment of physical conditions where there is probably a strong psychological element. Examples are psychosomatic illnesses such as hysterical paralysis or kleptomania, or conditions caused by stress such as migraines, nail-biting, bed-wetting, eating disorders and skin problems. The therapy is also recommended for treating problems in the gastro-intestinal tract, such as colitis, which are thought to be stress-related. It has also proved effective in treating insomnia and anxiety as well as phobias, such as fear of spiders, exams, heights or flying, and addictions and dependency states, such as alcoholism, smoking and gambling. In dentistry, the technique is used for analgesia.

Practising hypnotherapy

Most hypnotherapists work either on their own or in private practice, but there is increasing scope for working in hospitals. Hypnotherapy has not yet been regulated and it is very important to receive proper training from a recognized institution. Contact either the Association of Ethical and Professional Hypnotherapists or the National Register of Hypnotherapists and Psychotherapists or the National School of Hypnosis and Psychotherapy for details of education and training.

Osteopathy

Osteopathy is a system of manipulating the bones and tissues to relieve pain and tension. The osteopath corrects dysfunctional movements in the body and allows the natural healing to take place. Many people think of osteopaths as people who may cure their backache when all else has failed, but osteopathy can have more far-reaching results. Although a lot of the treatment is concerned with manipulation of the spine, it can extend to the whole of the body and provide benefit in cases of apparently unrelated illness. Recent research suggests that muscular and skeletal disorders can create abnormal strains on nerves and blood vessels, which, in turn, can have an effect on such functions as digestion, respiration and circulation. So, although the primary function of osteopaths is to relieve pain, they may also be able to alleviate a wider range of disorders.

Practising osteopathy

If you decide to practise this form of therapy, you will use a complex system of manipulation for which you will need a sound knowledge of anatomy. Before you decide on a course of treatment, however, you will take a full case history of your patient, much as a doctor does, and make a full clinical examination of the patient's present condition. You will note the configuration of the spine and test the patient's ability to walk and move his or her limbs. Only when you have all the necessary evidence, and are able to decide that manipulation will work, will you begin the appropriate course of treatment. Although manipulation can be helpful in many cases, there are disorders for which it would be disastrous, for instance if the prognosis is osteoporosis (brittle bones) or if the joints are inflamed. For this reason, basic clinical knowledge is needed for diagnostic purposes and, if you are in any doubt, you must refer your patient to someone who can provide the necessary backup. Training is rigorous and lasts for four or five years. Osteopathy is regulated by the Osteopathy Act 1993, so that unless you have recognized qualifications and credentials you cannot lawfully practise osteopathy in the UK. Contact the General Osteopathic Council for further details.

Case Study

John has been teaching yoga for many years and is now taking a part-time course in osteopathy.

During my years of yoga teaching I have been working out ways of opening up the body and freeing energy. What I do is to stretch people out and achieve a very deep, very powerful stretching of the muscles. When I am qualified as an osteopath I will combine this with osteopathic techniques. It is interesting work – everything comes into it, including psychology. You can't divorce bones from the brain. The idea is seeing someone as a total person. I believe that the body has its own healing force and for this reason I see education as my primary function. I teach exercises first and do manipulation second. Only in cases of extreme pain is manipulation the priority.

Many people become ill because they have no safety valves. My job is to teach people how to relax deeply – both physically and mentally. Most people don't even know how to breathe. PE in schools would be an opportunity for this kind of education, but in fact no one teaches you about your body and how to keep it functioning.

Most patients who come to osteopaths do not need much medical diagnosis but there are always the exceptions. As well as the osteopathic, or structural diagnosis, the osteopath is qualified to make a medical diagnosis, but obviously doctors are better at it because they are doing it all the time. There ought to be much more contact between the two sectors, much more working together. That would be the best hope for the future.

Reflexology

Reflexology treats the whole body through massage applied to specific pressure points in both feet. The feet are seen to reflect the condition of specific parts of the body. Practitioners believe that 'energy channels' connect the feet with parts of the body, and that health problems stem from blockages in these energy channels. The massage unblocks the channels to restart the flow of energy so that healing without the use of drugs or surgery can occur. The treatment can be used to alleviate a very wide range of conditions, including acne, asthma, depression, hormonal imbalances, loss of libido, neck pain, rheumatism, stiffness and stress.

Practising reflexology

Reflexology is unregulated in the UK, which means that you have to be careful to find a reputable training establishment. Contact the Association of Reflexologists, which runs courses that are government approved, or the equally reputable British Reflexology Association, for further details.

Yoga

Many medical practitioners as well as alternative therapists are becoming increasingly interested in yoga with its emphasis on awareness and control of both body and mind. There are different types of yoga with very many yoga techniques. Regular practice provides many benefits such as enhanced concentration, increased energy and stamina and toned-up muscles. The aim of therapeutic yoga has traditionally been to promote and maintain a healthy mind and body, although it has more recently been used to treat symptoms of disease.

Practising yoga

It is very important to find a reputable training establishment. Contact either the British Wheel of Yoga or the Iyengar Yoga Institute for further details.

8 Mental health

Introduction

The field of mental health is wide and difficult to define. Problems may range from temporary emotional difficulties to physiological learning difficulties. In general the area is characterized by being very labour intensive and staffed by people who have trained in a variety of disciplines. Treatment is provided in a number of different settings funded by several agencies.

Treatment of mental health difficulties has traditionally followed particular theoretical models. The key models, which differ widely in their approach to particular problems, are the following:

- The medical model, which views mental disorders as *illnesses* which can be physiologically tested.
- The cognitive model, which sees disorders as arising through *negative thought patterns*. Treatment centres on challenging negative thoughts.
- The behavioural model, which does not speculate on mental processes at all; rather, it selects only observable *behaviour* as the problem. Treatment centres on reinforcing appropriate behaviours.
- The social model, which investigates underlying *social causes* (for example, divorce, poor housing). Treatment requires changes in living conditions.

◆ The psychodynamic model, which views repressed *unconscious conflicts* as the source of the disorder. Treatment involves making these hidden conflicts conscious.

In general, the mental health professions follow on from these theoretical models, although in recent years there has been a move by all who operate in the field towards integration and the development of eclectic methods to obtain the best treatment most relevant for a particular client.

While the work you do will be dictated to an extent by the setting, it will vary according to your training and personal inclinations.

Work settings

As with other forms of health provision, treatment is given in two main settings: in hospitals and in the community. Following the Mental Health Act 1983, the overwhelming trend is a move to work in the community with a closure of long-term mental hospitals. This applies to all forms of care, from emotional problems to people with learning difficulties. The health, education and social services, a variety of voluntary associations and the private sector provide services. Each tends to employ people who have trained within a particular discipline, though this is not an absolute rule.

Training and professional functions

The main functions practised within mental health are assessment, counselling and various forms of psychotherapy, and drug and ECT treatment. People come to the work through the following routes.

Psychiatrists are medically qualified people who choose to specialize in psychiatry. They follow the postgraduate training pattern described in Chapter 3 and take the membership examination of the Royal College of Psychiatrists (MRC Psych). In accordance with the Mental Health Act, many psychiatrists now work in community teams. It is quite common for psychiatrists to take a further training in psychoanalysis at a later stage in their career.

Psychotherapists work in situations where treatment is given through some kind of talking, whether one-to-one, with family units, or in groups. They concern themselves with understanding the problems within the individual's psyche, or a family's relationships, or with group dynamics. A common training for psychotherapy is a degree in Humanities, followed by a professional training. This always entails a course of personal insight training or analysis and many people come to the work because of their own experience of such therapy. Doctors wishing to become psychotherapists will receive postgraduate training (and advice on it) through the training structure described in Chapter 3.

Recent developments in psychotherapy include brief, time-limited psychotherapies available within the NHS. Cognitive Analytic Therapy (CAT), for example, is an integrative therapy which uses an eclectic mix of cognitive, psychoanalytic and behavioural strategies to enable clients to develop specific tools with which a person can understand and change maladaptive coping patterns. CAT has been used in many NHS settings, ranging from general mental health to specialist, forensic and eating disorders. Currently, CAT training is rapidly expanding throughout the UK. Another psychotherapy, psychosynthesis, works towards integrating different therapeutic methods, with a particular emphasis on the concept of 'the will'.

Psychologists are graduates in psychology who have taken further professional training to become either clinical or educational psychologists. Work experience is necessary before embarking on any professional training; for educational psychologists this must be in teaching while for clinical psychologists work experience requires clinical psychiatric experience. Psychologists have, until recently, been concerned mainly with assessment and testing and have therefore worked largely in an advisory capacity with those people actually giving treatment. Historically there has been a tendency for psychologists to work with people who have emotional problems, using behavioural and cognitive techniques. Psychologists can be employed in a variety of settings, but are usually taken on by the health or education authorities.

Unlike other practitioners in the mental health field, psychologists are equipped to develop new treatment strategies. Behavioural operant conditioning methods for people with learning difficulties are a recent development that has proved highly successful for reducing problem behaviours.

Psychiatric social workers are people with social work qualifications who can choose to specialize in mental health by taking additional professional training. Such people often work in community settings where their background enables them to work with whole families. Unlike other workers in the health-care professions, social workers have important legal powers and responsibilities. These particularly concern work with children where, for example, social workers may be required to take out care orders to restrict parent access.

Counsellors are often employed in educational establishments, giving advice and backup to students with personal problems and working mainly on the level of interpersonal relationships. Many are trained teachers who may have taken one of the counselling courses available. Counsellors are employed under various guises. Some are called counsellors, some are known as young people's advisers, and others fulfil this function within the wider brief of the post of education welfare officer.

Outside education, job opportunities are limited in the present economic climate, though there is a demand for part-time voluntary counsellors to work with community groups dealing with a wide range of problems.

Working in hospitals

Hospitals divide into two main groups: those dealing with learning difficulties and mental illness, whether chronic or acute, and general hospitals which have departments of psychiatry often handling less severe cases, mainly in the outpatient clinic. The work encountered in the two groups will be very different and the nature of the work will depend both on the problems presented by individual patients and on the perceptions and aims of the staff dealing with them. Long-term in-patient work has been radically changed by the effects of the Mental Health Act 1983 and the multidisciplinary team approach whereby particular therapeutic roles and responsibilities (such as drugs, psychotherapy and behavioural work) are allocated to particular members of the team.

Case Study

A child and family psychiatrist reviews her work

Ruth *combined her training with raising a young family, and now, 13 years after she qualified, is looking for a part-time consultancy.*

I went into medicine because I had an interest in people's emotions and ideas about treating the whole person. As a student I was very involved in psychiatry during two out of three of my clinical years. We had a well-known psychoanalyst teaching at the time and he had a great personal influence on me. He was very uncompromising in his approach and insisted that we gain a helpful understanding of *all* aspects of the patient's life. We also did some individual psychotherapy under supervision.

When I qualified, initially I was intending to go into general medicine as a route to psychiatry, but the next thing that happened was that I became pregnant and did a job in paediatrics all at the same time. I decided to combine my two interests and go into child psychiatry but the great question was: how? That was 12 years ago, and at that time the training structure was only thinly mapped out. As hospital posts were virtually an impossibility for me I felt at a standstill and didn't know how to pursue what I knew I ultimately wanted to do. I took up the opportunity of doing some sessions in paediatrics, which were quite useful on the developmental side, and then, two years later, had my second child. After that I spent two years working on a research project on developmental paediatrics and emotional problems, got the project published, and became a school doctor. By this time, it was obvious to me that the pathway to child psychology was via adult psychiatry, which is concerned mainly with mental illness rather than with people with problems. My third child was born around this time and I got myself a part-time registrar post in a mental hospital. With a gap for maternity leave, I carried on with this part-time training both in the mental hospital and in a district general hospital for three years. During this time I took my MRC Psych and then was appointed to a part-time senior registrar post in child psychiatry, in which I have been for the past four years.

My main interest now is in family therapy. There's a lot of unexploited scope to help people with problems mainly through talking and looking at the family and social environment. Most children are referred because of disturbing emotional states such as unhappiness or anxiety, for behavioural problems like stealing, disobedience or truancy, or because they present bodily symptoms – soiling, abdominal pains, eczema, asthma, and so forth. It is very common to express emotional difficulties in these ways. As I see it, there's usually no point in treating the symptoms – you have to go back to what got them there. That's why I like working with the whole family, because they are all likely to be involved.

Case Study

A talk with a consultant child psychiatrist

I work in a rural area, and am one of three consultant child psychiatrists in the county. There are nine consultants in adult psychiatry and, although our work areas do not usually overlap, we all cooperate over on-call duties. Otherwise, my time is divided between a residential child psychiatric unit, a hospital for the mentally subnormal, two sessions working in social services assessment centres, and the remainder in outpatient clinics of local hospitals.

It is a working life with a lot of variety, and I think this is one of the attractive aspects of psychiatry. I am working not only in different settings but also with people as individuals, and no two people are alike. So the work is non-repetitive. I also work with multidisciplinary teams and we each bring our own expertise to bear on the problems our patients present.

My main involvement is with the child psychiatric unit. We take between 24 and 40 children from the age of 5 until 19, and aim to provide them with an environment for living in which their problems can be treated. All have fairly extreme forms of psychosis or neurosis. We have family accommodation, at present occupied by a mother and her six-year-old son, which enables us to treat a family as a unit when other forms of treatment have failed or simply to offer accommodation to parents should they wish it. We also have a school, which the children attend, and a team of workers consisting of myself, nursing staff, social workers, therapists and teachers. We discuss each child every six weeks with the parents present, and together we decide how treatment should proceed. We don't work according to set theories. We are open-minded and will try anything that we think will prove effective.

The mental subnormality hospital has a preponderance of adults. There is an increasing tendency for handicapped children to be cared for in the community, which means that those remaining in the hospital are mainly very severely handicapped. The hospital is divided into two units, and I have responsibility for one of them, both adults and children. My role is one of general medical and psychiatric supervision of the team of workers, in the sense of both general and individual management of patients, their treatment and training programmes.

Working in the community

The main forms of mental health care in the community are provided by the health, education and social services, MIND, a variety of voluntary bodies (notably Arbours and Relate), and by private clinics. Recently, there has been a sharp increase in growth in provision of services in the community. The move to the community was intended to provide less stigmatized and more integrated facilities than the old 'asylums' could provide. In some instances, however, shortages of funds have resulted in diminished standards of care. The work takes place in child guidance clinics, health centres, family welfare clinics, educational establishments, some general practices and clinics run privately or by voluntary bodies. In the case of people employed by health authorities, there are many areas of overlap between hospital- and community-based work. Psychiatrists and psychologists, for instance, may be attached to a hospital but do much of their work in a community setting. The methods of treatment are similar to in-patient work, although it is hoped that the stigma and isolation of the hospital will be avoided. However, the lack of availability of provision of treatment (such as drugs and coun-selling) owing to depleted funds has been a major issue of concern.

Case Study

A psychotherapist discusses her work

Pam *works for a voluntary group providing various forms of psycho-therapy for women within a feminist framework.*

Our group started life in a basement through the initiative of two feminists who saw a need for a provision specifically for women. They advertised in the feminist journals and the response was overwhelming.

Now, there are five therapists and new premises with six rooms – two for group work and four for individual therapy. We are financed mainly by fees, which we charge on a sliding scale, but we do have some funding from Partnerships and various charitable trusts which enables us to widen the scope of our work and undertake projects which are broadly 'educational'.

Our work is mainly of five types. We offer long- and short-term therapy, organize workshops, start and support self-help groups and run training courses for people already working in the field. We find the greatest demand is for individual therapy, either to help women with ongoing problems or to assist in the short term with people experiencing crises. Workshops are usually theme-related, under headings such as 'Women and Anger', 'Mothers and Children', or 'Sexuality', and in self-help groups we have done a lot of work on compulsive eating. We also help mixed groups of women who want a structure for getting together and sorting out their problems. We see our training courses as a topping-up for people who are already trained. Our view is that to train as a therapist you must train broadly, and we, after all, are specialists.

Nowadays there is a choice of professional training courses run by places like the Tavistock Clinic and Arbours, but when I trained, these weren't in existence. I took a Mental Health course at the LSE. This entailed doing therapy under supervision and having personal analysis. Until I came here I worked in NHS clinics as a psychotherapist, and much of my work here has been in psychotherapy. At the moment I am developing my interest in counselling, which is concerned with interpersonal relationships as opposed to problems within the psyche. I am planning a course on 'Counselling by Women for Women' – obviously a woman-to-woman counselling relationship is very different from a man-to-woman one, and I want to explore this through the course.

We have expanded, but still cannot cope with the demand. There are good places where adults seeking individual therapy can go, both under the NHS and privately, but finding them can be very difficult – rather like looking for a needle in a haystack.

Case Study

An education welfare officer reviews her job

Sue *is a school-attached worker and deals with secondary school age pupils who have no school counsellor. She therefore provides this service.*

I operate in two distinct ways: as a worker with families who are usually referred to me for truancy problems, and as a counsellor for children with personal problems. I took this job after completing teacher training so I have learnt my counselling techniques on the job. The Authority runs an induction course but I didn't find it very useful.

The teaching staff refers some children to me, but often children come to me of their own accord because I am in a neutral position and they can expect confidentiality. This is very important. They do not want their teachers to know about the things that they tell me. I get all sorts of problems thrown at me. A child will burst in, saying, 'Please help me, I never want to go home again.' Some are quite disturbed – temporarily. Most problems boil down to conflicts with parents or difficulties in sexual relationships. I never take a moralistic standpoint, although if I am asked straight out what I think, I will give an opinion.

I prefer to spend the first few sessions getting children to talk out the problem, offering some suggestions for ways of thinking about it so that perhaps they will analyze it and find solutions themselves. Very often these problems have common-sense answers. Occasionally I will set specific tasks, especially in cases involving conflicts that arise for particular reasons. I will, for instance, ask a child who is clashing with parents because of untidiness to be especially tidy for one week and see how that changes the situation. I will also give advice if this seems appropriate.

The patterns of self-referral are interesting. Girls will come alone to see me; boys come in groups, full of bravado, and will very rarely admit to problems. They have obviously come for a reason, but it is very difficult to break through and identify it.

A large part of this job is recognizing problems. You have to be able to make a quick assessment – is it a personal, educational or social problem or do the problems, in fact, overlap? You have to be able to judge when you can help and when you should refer to another agency. We need to know a little about a lot!

Salary scales

Pay generally relates more to the training and discipline rather than to the mode or style of work you are doing. The disciplines of psychiatry, psychology and social work have their own career and pay structures on a national basis. Counselling, psychotherapy and psychoanalysis have pay structures more determined by fund-holder offers or private personalized charge rates.

Finding a job

Write to the address of the professional association of the discipline you are interested in or phone for further information (see Chapter 9 pp 115–18 under the Mental Health section for organizations in the field). Most job advertisements appear in the journals of the various professional associations. It is also advisable to look at Wednesday's *Guardian* and on hospital billboards. The best way to find a job is often through networking with professional colleagues.

 **Contact points**

General

Universities and Colleges Admissions Service (UCAS)
Rosehill
New Barn Lane
Cheltenham
Gloucestershire GL52 3LZ
Tel: (01242) 227788
Web: www.ucas.ac.uk

The Educational Grants Advisory Service
c/o Family Welfare Association
501–505 Kingsland Road
London E8 4AU
Tel: (020) 7254 6251

Chapters 2 and 3   Medicine

General

British Medical Association (BMA)
BMA House
Tavistock Square
London WC1H 9JP
Tel: (020) 7387 4499

British Medical Association (BMA)
Bartree House
460 Palatine Road
Northenden M22 4DJ
Tel: (0161) 945 8989
Web: www.bma.org.uk

Department of Postgraduate Medicine and Dentistry
Gateway House
Piccadilly South
Manchester M60 7LP
Tel: (0161) 237 2091
Web: www.pgmd.man.ac.uk

General Medical Council
178–202 Great Portland Street
London W1N 6JE
Tel: (020) 7580 7642

British Medical Association Education Trust
BMA House
Tavistock Square
London WC1H 9JP
Tel: (020) 7387 4499

Medical Women's Federation
Tavistock House North
Tavistock Square
London WC1H 9HX
Tel: (020) 7387 7765
Web: www.m–w–f.demon.co.uk

Public Health Laboratory Service (HQ)
61 Colindale Avenue
London NW9 5HT
Tel: (020) 8200 1295
Web: www.phls.co.uk

Medical schools

ABERDEEN
University of Aberdeen
Aberdeen AB24 3FX
Tel: (01224) 272031
Web: www.abdn.ac.uk
AAB (A levels), AAAAB (Scottish Highers), AAAAAB (Irish
Leaving Certificate), 5yFT

BELFAST
Queen's University of Belfast
University Road
Belfast BT7 1NN
Tel: (028) 9033 5081
Web: www.qub.ac.uk
e-mail: admissions@qub.ac.uk
AAA (A levels), AAAABB (Irish Leaving Certificate), 5yFT

BIRMINGHAM
University of Birmingham
Edgbaston
Birmingham B15 2TT
Tel: (0121) 414 3344
Web: www.bham.ac.uk
AAB (A levels), AAAAAB (Irish Leaving Certificate), 5yFT

BRISTOL
School of Medical Sciences
University Walk
Bristol BS8 1TD
Tel: (0117) 928 8625
Web: www.medeci.bris.ac.uk/directions.asp
ABB (A levels), 5yFT

CAMBRIDGE
Cambridge University
Cambridge Intercollegiate
Kellett Lodge
Tennis Court Road
Cambridge CB2 1QJ
Tel: (01223) 333308
Web: www.cam.ac.uk
AAA (A levels), 5yFT

DUNDEE
University of Dundee
Dundee DD1 4HN
Tel: (01382) 344160
Web: www.dundee.ac.uk
ABB (A levels), AAABB (Scottish Highers), AAAAAA (Irish
Leaving Certificate), 5yFT

EDINBURGH
University of Edinburgh
Edinburgh EH8 9YL
Tel: (0131) 650 1000
Web: www.ed.ac.uk
AAB (A levels), AAAAB (Scottish Highers), AAAAAA (Irish
Leaving Certificate), 5yFT

GLASGOW
University of Glasgow
Glasgow G12 8QQ
Tel: (0141) 330 4575
Web: www.gla.ac.uk
AAB (A levels), AAAAB (Scottish Highers), AAAABB (Irish
Leaving Certificate), 5yFT

IRELAND
Faculty of Health Sciences
Chemistry Building
Trinity College
Dublin 2
Tel: (353) 1 608 1476

Faculty of Medicine
Ardpatrick
College Road
University College
Cork
Tel: (353) 21 490 2272
Web: www.ucc.ie/ucc/faculties/medical/index.html

LEEDS
University of Leeds
Leeds LS2 9JT
Tel: (0113) 233 3999
Web: www.leeds.ac.uk
AAB (A levels), AAAAB (Scottish Highers), AAAABB (Irish
Leaving Certificate), 5yFT

LEICESTER
University of Leicester
University Road
Leicester LE1 7RH
Tel: (0116) 252 5281
Web: www.le.ac.uk
AAB (A levels), AAAAA (Irish Leaving Certificate), 5yFT

LIVERPOOL
University of Liverpool
P O Box 147
Liverpool L69 3BX
Tel: (0151) 794 2000
Web: www.liv.ac.uk
AAB (A levels), 5yFT

LONDON
Guy's, King's and St Thomas' School of Medicine
Management Suite
First Floor, Hodgkin Building
Guy's Campus
London SE1 9RT
Tel: (020) 7848 6971
Web: www.chms.ac.uk/schlweb.htm
AAB (A levels), 5yFT

Imperial College of Science, Technology and Medicine
(including St Mary's)
South Kensington
London SW7 2AZ
Tel: (020) 7594 8014
Web: www.ic.ac.uk
e-mail: admissions@ic.ac.uk
ABB (A levels), 6yFT

St Bartholemew's
Royal London School of Medicine
Queen Mary and Westfield College
Turner Street
London E1 2AD
Tel: (020) 7377 7611
ABB (A levels), 5–6yFT

St George's Hospital Medical School
Crammer Terrace
London SW17 0RE
Tel: (020) 8725 5992
Web: www.sghms.ac.uk
AAA (A levels), 5yFT

University College (including the Royal Free)
Gower Street
London WC1E 6BT
Tel: (020) 7380 7365
e-mail: degree-info@ucl.ac.uk
AAB (A levels), 6yFT

MANCHESTER
Faculty of Medicine, Dentistry and Nursing
University of Manchester
Stopford Building
Oxford Road
Manchester M13 9PT
Tel: (0161) 275 5027
Web: www.medicine.man.ac.uk
ABB (A levels), 5–6yFT

NOTTINGHAM
University of Nottingham
University Park
Nottingham NG7 2RD
Tel: (0115) 951 6565
Web: www.nottingham.ac.uk
AAB (A levels), 5yFT

OXFORD
Oxford University
College Admissions Office
Wellington Square
Oxford OX1 2JD
Tel: (01865) 270207
Web: www.ox.ac.uk
AAA (A levels), AAAAA (Scottish Highers), AAAABB (Irish
Leaving Certificate), 6yFT

ST ANDREWS
University of St Andrews
College Gate
St Andrews KY16 9AJ
Tel: (01334) 462150
Web: www.st-and.ac.uk
ABB (A levels), AAABB (Scottish Highers), AAAAA (Irish
Leaving Certificate), 5yFT

SHEFFIELD
University of Sheffield
Sheffield S10 2TN
Tel: (0114) 271 2142
Web: www.shef.ac.uk
ABB (A levels), 5yFT

SOUTHAMPTON
University of Southampton
Southampton SO17 1BJ
Tel: (023) 8059 5000
Web: www.soton.ac.uk
e-mail: admissns@soton.ac.uk
ABB (A levels), 5yFT

WALES
University College of Wales
College of Medicine
Undergraduate Admissions Office
Health Park
Cardiff CF4 4XN
Tel: (029) 2074 2027
Web: www.uwcm.ac.uk
AAB (A levels), 6yFT

Royal Colleges

ACCIDENT AND EMERGENCY
Faculty of Accident and Emergency Medicine
35–43 Lincoln's Inn Fields
London EC4V 6EJ
Tel: (020) 831 9405

ANAESTHETISTS
Royal College of Anaesthetists
48–49 Russell Square
London WC1B 4JY
Tel: (020) 7813 1900

OBSTETRICS AND GYNAECOLOGY
Royal College of Obstetricians and Gynaecologists
27 Sussex Place
Regent's Park
London NW1 4RG
Tel: (020) 262 5425

OCCUPATIONAL MEDICINE
Faculty of Occupational Medicine of the Royal College of
Physicians
6 St Andrew's Place
Regent's Park
London NW1 4LB
Tel: (020) 7487 3414

OPHTHALMOLOGISTS
Royal College of Ophthalmologists
17 Cornwall Terrace
London NW1 4QW
Tel: (020) 7935 0702
Web: www.rcophth.ac.uk

PAEDIATRICS AND CHILD HEALTH
Royal College of Paediatrics and Child Health
50 Hallam Street
London W1N 6DE
Tel: (020) 7307 5600
e-mail: enquiries@rcpch.ac.uk

PATHOLOGISTS
Royal College of Pathologists
2 Carlton House Terrace
London SW1Y 5AF
Tel: (020) 930 5861

PHARMACEUTICAL MEDICINE
Faculty of Pharmaceutical Medicine of the Royal College of
Physicians of the United Kingdom
1 St Andrew's Place
Regent's Park
London NW1 4LB
Tel: (020) 7224 0343

PHYSICIANS
Royal College of Physicians
11 St Andrew's Place
Regent's Park
London NW1 4LE
Tel: (020) 7935 1174

PSYCHIATRISTS
Royal College of Psychiatrists
17 Belgrave Square
London SW1X 8PG
Tel: (020) 7235 2351

RADIOLOGISTS
Royal College of Radiologists
38 Portland Place
London W1N 4JQ
Tel: (020) 7636 4432

SURGEONS
Royal College of Surgeons of England
35–43 Lincoln's Inn Fields
London WC2A 3PN
Tel: (020) 7405 3474

Financial support

NHS Student Grants Unit
Room 212C Government Buildings
Norcross
Blackpool FY5 3TA
Tel: (01253) 856123

Department of Education for Northern Ireland
Rathgael House
Bangor Road
Bangor
County Down BP19 7PR
Tel: (028) 9127 9418

Student Awards Agency in Scotland
3 Redhenghs Rigg
South Gyle
Edinburgh EH12 9HH
Tel: (0131) 556 8400

Welsh Health Common Services Agency
Education Purchasing Unit
Ground Floor CP2
Welsh Office
Cathays Park
Cardiff CF1 3NQ
Tel: (029) 2082 5111

Chapter 4   General practitioners

General

Royal College of General Practitioners
14 Princess Gate
London SW7 1PU
Tel: (020) 7581 3232
e-mail: info@rcgp.org.uk

Faculty of Public Health Medicine of the Royal Colleges of
Physicians of the United Kingdom
4 St Andrew's Place
London NW1 4LB
Tel: (020) 7935 0243

Regional Postgraduate GP Directors and Deans

EAST ANGLIA
Dr A Hibble
The General Practice Office
Postgraduate Medical and Dental Education
East Anglia Deanery
Block 3 Ida Darwin Site
Fulbourn
Cambridge CB1 5EE
Tel: (01223) 884848

EAST SCOTLAND
Dr D Snadden
Department of General Practice
Tayside Centre for General Practice
Kirsty Semple Way
Charleston Drive
Dundee DD2 4AD
Tel: (01382) 632771
Web: www.dundee.ac.uk/generalpractice

MERSEY
Dr A G Mathie
Postgraduate GP Office
Hamilton House
24 Pall Mall
Liverpool L3 6AL
Tel: (0151) 236 2637

NORTH EAST SCOTLAND
Dr M Taylow
Aberdeen Postgraduate Centre
Medical School
Foresterhill
Aberdeen AB9 2ZD
Tel: (01224) 681818 ext 53976

NORTHERN
Professor T van Zwanenberg
10–12 Framlington Place
The University
Newcastle NE2 4AB
Tel: (0191) 222 7029
Web: www.ncl.ac.uk/pimd

NORTHERN IRELAND
Dr A McKnight
Northern Ireland Council for Postgraduate Education
5 Annadale Avenue
Belfast BT7 3JH
Tel: (028) 9049 2731

NORTH SCOTLAND
Dr H I McNamara
North of Scotland Institute of Postgraduate Medical Education
Raigmore Hospital
Inverness IV2 3UJ
Tel: (01463) 705201
Web: www.inverness-pgmc.demon.co.uk

NORTH THAMES (WEST)
Professor P Pietron
Ground Floor
Courtfield House
St Charles Hospital
Exmoor Street
London W10 6DZ
Tel: (020) 8962 4680

NORTH WESTERN
Dr W J D McKinlay
Department of Postgraduate Medical Studies
Gateway House
Piccadilly South
Manchester M60 7LP
Tel: (0161) 237 2104
Web: www.pgmd.man.ac.uk

OXFORD
Dr N Johnson
Oxford PGMDE
The Triangle
Roosevelt Drive
Headington
Oxford OX3 7XP
Tel: (01865) 740644

SOUTH EAST SCOTLAND
Dr D Blaney
Lister Postgraduate Institute
11 Hill Square
Edinburgh EH8 9DR
Tel: (0131) 650 8085

SOUTH THAMES (EAST)
Dr A Tavabie
9th Floor
Capital House
42 Weston Street
London SE1 3QD
Tel: (020) 7940 9100

SOUTH THAMES (WEST)
Professor R G Hornung
Department of Postgraduate GP Education
2 Stirling House Stirling Road
Guildford GU2 5RF
Tel: (01483) 579492

SOUTH WESTERN
Professor Sir D J Pereira Gray
Institute of General Practice
Postgraduate Medical School
Barrack Road
Exeter EX2 5DW
Tel: (01392) 403006
Web: www.swesterndeanery.demon.co.uk

TRENT
Dr P Lane
Postgraduate Dean's Office
University of Sheffield School of Medicine
Beech Hill Road
Sheffield S10 2RX
Tel: (0114) 271 2526

Dr J Dilkhu
Postgraduate Office
Medical School
Queen's Medical Centre
Nottingham, NG7 2UH
Tel: (0115) 970 9377

Dr D Sowden
Postgraduate Education Department
Leicester General Hospital
Gwendolen Road
Leicester LE5 4PW
Tel: (0116) 258 8119

WALES
Dr S A Smail
Department of Postgraduate Medicine and Dentistry
University of Wales College of Medicine
Health Park
Cardiff CF4 4XN
Tel: (029) 2074 3059
Web: www.PrimaryCare.uwcm.ac.uk

WESSEX
Dr F Smith
Postgraduate Medical and Dental Education
Highcroft
Romsey Road
Winchester
Hampshire S022 5DH
Tel: (01962) 863511 ext 845
Web: www.wesswx.org.uk

WEST MIDLANDS
Dr S Field
Postgraduate Medical and Dental Education
West Midlands
NHS Executive
27 Highfield Road
Edgbaston
Birmingham B15 3DP
Tel: (0121) 456 5600

WEST SCOTLAND
Professor T S Murray
West of Scotland Postgraduate Medical Education Board
1 Hoselethill Road
Glasgow G12 9LX
Tel: (0141) 339 8855 ext 5276
Web: www.gla.ac.uk/Acad/PGMed

YORKSHIRE
Dr J Bahrami
Department of Postgraduate Medical Education
Willow Terrace Road
University of Leeds
Leeds LS2 9JT
Tel: (0113) 233 1517
Web: www.cmeplus.co.uk

Public health

Faculty of Public Health Medicine
4 St Andrew's Place
London NW1 4LB
Tel: (020) 7935 0243
e-mail: candakincses@fphm.org.uk

Chapter 5   Dentistry

General

British Association of Dental Therapists
C/o the Dental Auxiliary School
University Dental Hospital
Heath Park
Cardiff CF4 4XY
Tel: (029) 2074 4685

British Dental Association
64 Wimpole Street
London W1M 8AL
Tel: (020) 7935 0875

British Dental Hygienists' Association
C/o School of Dental Hygiene
University Dental Hospital
Higher Cambridge Street
Manchester M15 6FH
Tel: (0161) 275 6711

British Society of Paediatric Dentistry
e-mail: Densaf@leeds.ac.uk

Faculty of General Dental Practitioners
Royal College of Surgeons
35–43 Lincoln's Inn Fields
London WC2A 3PNI
Tel: (020) 7405 3474

General Dental Council
37 Wimpole Street
London W1M 8DQ
Tel: (020) 887 3800

Irish Dental Council
57 Merrion Square
Dublin 2
Eire
Tel: (353) 1 676 2226

National Advice Centre for Postgraduate Dental Education
C/o Faculty of Dental Surgery
Royal College of Surgeons of England
35–43 Lincoln's Inn Fields
London WC2A 3PN
Tel: (020) 7973 2181

Dental schools

(Pre-dental schools are marked with an asterisk. The usual A level or other requirements are given after the addresses and phone numbers.)

*ABERTAY, DUNDEE
Dental School
Park Place
Dundee DD1 4HN
Tel: (01382) 660111
Web: www.dundee.ac.uk/dentalschool
ABB (Scottish Highers AAAAB)

BELFAST
School of Clinical Dentistry
Queen's University of Belfast
Royal Victoria Hospital
Grosvenor Road
Belfast BT12 6BP
Tel: (028) 8024 503 ext 2733/2734
AAB (Scottish Highers AAAAB)

BIRMINGHAM
Dental School
The Dental School
Birmingham University
St Chad's Queensway
Birmingham B4 6NN
Tel: (0121) 236 8611
ABB (Scottish Highers AAAAB)

*BRISTOL
Dental School
Bristol University
Lower Maudlin Street
Bristol BS1 2LY
Tel: (0117) 928 4308
Web: www.dent.bris.ac.uk
ABB (Scottish Highers AAAAB)

IRELAND
Cork Dental School and Hospital
Wilton
Cork
Tel: (35321) 545100

Dublin Dental Hospital
Lincoln Place
Dublin
Tel: (35316) 127200

GLASGOW
Glasgow Dental Hospital
378 Sauchiehall Street
Glasgow G2 3JZ
Tel: (0141) 211 9600
Web: www.gla.ac.uk/Acad/Dental.html
ABB (Scottish Highers AAAAB)

LEEDS
School of Dentistry
University of Leeds
Clarendon Way
Leeds LS2 9LU
Tel: (0113) 233 6199
Web: www.leeds.ac.uk/dental/dental.html
BBB (Scottish Highers AAABB)

LIVERPOOL
School of Dental Surgery
Liverpool University
Pembroke Place
PO Box 147
Liverpool L69 3BX
Tel: (0151) 706 5201
Web: www.liv.ac.uk/luds/front/index.html
ABB (Scottish Highers AAAAB)

LONDON
Guy's, King's College and St Thomas' Hospital Medical and
Dental School
St Thomas Street
London Bridge SE1 9RT
Tel: (020) 7955 5000
Web: www.umds.ac.uk
BBB (Scottish Highers AAAAB)

St Bartholomew's and the Royal London School of Medicine
and Dentistry
London Hospital Medical College
Dental School
Turner Street
London E1 2AD
Tel: (020) 7377 7000
Web: www.mds.qmw.ac.uk
BBB (Scottish Highers AAAAB)

Eastman Dental Institute for Oral Health Care Sciences
University of London
256 Gray's Inn Road
London WC1X 8LD
Tel: (020) 7915 1038
e-mail: dean@eastman.ucl.ac.uk – postgraduate admissions
only.
(Each London dental school counts as a separate choice on the
UCAS application form.)

*MANCHESTER
Turner Dental School
Higher Cambridge Street
Manchester M15 6FH
Tel: (0161) 275 6671/6642
Web: www.den.man.ac.uk
ABB (Scottish Highers AAABB)

*NEWCASTLE
Dental School
Framlington Place
Newcastle upon Tyne NE2 4BW
Tel: (0191) 222 6732/8347
Web: www.newcastle.ac.uk/dental.html
ABB (Scottish Highers AAB minimum)

*SHEFFIELD
School of Clinical Dentistry
University of Sheffield
Claremont Crescent
Sheffield S10 2TA
Tel: (0114) 271 7801
ABB (Scottish Highers AAABB)

*WALES
Dental School
University of Wales
College of Medicine
Dental School
Heath Park
Cardiff CF4 4XY
Tel: (029) 2074 4277
BBB (Scottish Highers AAAAB)

Regional Postgraduate Dental Deans

BELFAST
D F Saunders
Department of Paediatric and Preventative Dentistry
Royal Victoria Hospital
Grosvenor Road
Belfast BT12 6BP
Tel: (028) 9024 0503

BIRMINGHAM
Professor J W Frame
Director, Department of Oral Surgery and Oral Medicine
University of Birmingham
Dental School
St Chad's Queensway
Birmingham B4 6NN
Tel: (0121) 236 8611

BRISTOL
D Steel
Dental Postgraduate Department
Bristol Dental Hospital
Lower Maudlin Street
Bristol BS1 21Y
Tel: (0117) 928 4525

CAMBRIDGE
G T Cheney
Director, Regional Postgraduate Office
The Clinical School
Addenbrooke's Hospital
Hills Road
Cambridge CB2 2SP
Tel: (01223) 336715
e-mail: GTC22@medschl.ca.ac.uk

CARDIFF
Eric Nash
Director of Postgraduate Dental Education
Room 155
Dental School
Heath Park
Cardiff, CF4 4XY
Tel: (029) 2074 3962
Web: www.uwcm.ac.uk

GLASGOW
Dr J S Rennie
Director of Postgraduate Education
Glasgow Dental Hospital
378 Sauchiehall Street
Glasgow G2 3JZ
Tel: (0141) 211 9747

LEEDS
J P Ralph
Department for NHS Postgraduate Medical and Dental
Education
University of Leeds
Willow Terrace Road
Leeds LS2 9JT
Tel: (0113) 233 1527

LONDON
D Rule
Thames Postgraduate Medical and Dental Education
33 Millman Street
London WC1N 3EJ
Tel: (020) 8831 6222

MERSEYSIDE
Dr John Lilley
Ground Floor
Hamilton House
24 Pall Mall
Liverpool
Merseyside, L3 6AL
Tel: (0151) 285 2214
e-mail: Jdl@mdcpde.co.uk

NEWCASTLE
D Smith
The Dental School
10–12 Framlington Place
Newcastle upon Tyne NE2 4AB
Tel: (0191) 232 8511

OXFORD
R Juniper
Director, Level 3
John Radcliffe Hospital
Headingtron
Oxford OX3 9DU
Tel: (01865) 221402

SHEFFIELD
Professor P S Rothwell
School of Clinical Dentistry
Wellesley Road
Sheffield S10 2SZ
Tel: (0114) 271 7982

SOUTHAMPTON
R T Reed
South & West (Wessex) RHA
Highcroft
Romsey Road
Winchester
Hampshire S022 5DH
Tel: (023) 8083 6511
Web: www.wessex.org.uk/dental

Chapter 6   Armed Services and working abroad

Armed Services

Royal Air Force Medical Liaison Officer
D of R & S
RAF Cranwell
PO Box 1000
Sleaford
Lincolnshire NG34 8GZ
Web: www.raf-careers.com/content/medical/
medoff_cnt2.htm

Royal Army Medical Corps
Officer Recruiting
RHQ RAMC
Keogh Barracks
Ash Vale, Aldershot
Hampshire GU12 5RQ
Tel: (01252) 340307
e-mail: rhq.ramc@clara.net

Royal Naval Medical Service
Freepost PHQ3
Gosport
Hampshire P012 2BR
Tel: (023) 8072 7818
Web: www.royal-navy.mod.uk/rnmedical/mochap.htm

Working abroad

Christians Abroad
Suite 233
Bon Marché Centre
241–51 Ferndale Road
London SW9 8BJ
Tel: (020) 7346 5956
e-mail: admin@cabroad.org.uk

Christian Vocations
Holloway Street West
Lower Gornal
Dudley
West Midlands DY3 2DZ
Tel: (01902) 882836

Department for International Development
Abercrombie House
Eaglesham Road
East Kilbride
Glasgow G75 8EA
Tel: (01355) 844000

International Health Exchange
134 Lower Marsh
London SE1 7AE
Tel: (020) 7620 3333

Medical Missionary Association
157 Waterloo Road
London SE1 8XN
Tel: (020) 7790 1336

Medical Service Ministries
PO Box 35
Hailsham
East Sussex BN27 3XW
Tel: (01323) 849047

Voluntary Service Overseas (VSO)
The Enquiries Unit
317 Putney Bridge Road
London SW15 2PN
Tel: (020) 8780 2266
Web: www.vso.org.uk

Chapter 7   Alternative medicine

General

Centre for Complementary Health Studies
Amory Building
Rennes Drive
Exeter EX4 4RT
Tel: (01392) 244498

Council for Complementary and Alternative Medicine
63 Jeddo Road
London N12 9HQ
Tel: (020) 8735 0632

Guild of Complementary Practitioners
Liddell House
Liddell Close
Finchampstead
Berkshire RG40 4NS
Tel: (0118) 973 5757
Web: www.gcpnet.com

Institute for Complementary Medicine (ICM)
Unit 15
Tavern Quay
Commercial Centre
Rope Street, London SE16 1TX
Tel: (020) 7237 5165
Web: www.icmedicine.co.uk

Acupressure

British Acupuncture Council
63 Jeddo Road
London W12 9HQ
Tel: (020) 8735 0400
e-mail: info@acupuncture.org.uk

Acupuncture

British Acupuncture Council
63 Jeddo Road
London W12 9HQ
Tel: (020) 8735 0400
e-mail: info@acupuncture.org.uk

Alexander Technique

Society of Teachers of the Alexander Technique
20 London House
266 Fulham Road
London SW10 9EL
Tel: (020) 7351 0828
e-mail: enquiries@stat.org.uk

Aromatherapy

Aromatherapy Organizations Council
PO Box 19834
London SE25 6WF
Tel: (020) 8251 7912
Web: www.aromatherapy-uk.org

Chiropractic

General Chiropractic Council
344–54 Grays Inn Road
London WC1X 8BP
Tel: (020) 7713 5155
e-mail: enquiries@gcc-uk.org

Flower remedies

Dr Edward Bach Foundation
Mount Vernon
Sotwell
Wallingford
Oxfordshire OX10 0PZ
Tel: (01491) 834678

Healing

Confederation of Healing Organizations
The Red and White House
113 High Street
Berkhamstead
Hertfordshire HP4 2DJ
Tel: (01442) 870660

National Federation of Spiritual Healers
Old Manor Farm Studio
Church Street
Sunbury on Thames
Middlesex TW16 6RG
Tel: (01932) 783164
e-mail: office@nfsh.org.uk

Herbal medicine (Western)

National Institute of Medical Herbalists
56 Longbrook Street
Exeter EX4 6AH
Tel: (01392) 426022

Homoeopathy

Faculty of Homoeopathy
15 Clerkenwell Close
London EC1R 0AA
Tel: (020) 7566 7800
Web: www.trusthomeopathy.org

Society of Homoeopaths
4a Artizan Road
Northampton NN1 4HU
Tel: (01604) 621400
e-mail: info@homeopathy-soh.org

Hypnotherapy

Association of Ethical and Professional Hypnotherapists
181 The Downs
Harlow
Essex CM20 3RH
Tel: (01279) 425284
e-mail: aeph@dreams2reality.co.uk

National Register of Hypnotherapists and Psychotherapists
12 Cross Street
Nelson
Lancashire BB9 7EN
Tel: (01282) 699378

National School of Hypnosis and Psychotherapy
28 Finsbury Park Road
London N4 2JX
Tel: (020) 7359 6991

Osteopathy

General Osteopathic Council
Osteopathy House
776 Tower Bridge Road
London SE1 3LU
Tel: (020) 7357 6655
Web: www.osteopathy.org.uk

Reflexology

Association of Reflexologists
27 Old Gloucester Street
London WC1N 3XX
Tel: (0870) 5673320
e-mail: aor@reflexology.org

British Reflexology Association
Baley School of Reflexology
Monks Orchard
Whitbourne
Worcester WR6 5RB
Tel: (01886) 821207

Yoga

British Wheel of Yoga
1 Hamilton Place
Boston Road
Sleaford
Lincolnshire NG34 7ES
Tel: (01529) 306851
e-mail: wheelyoga@aol.com

Iyengar Yoga Institute
223a Randolph Avenue
London W9 1NL
Tel: (020) 7624 3080
Web: www.iyi.org.uk

Chapter 8   Mental Health

Association of Child Psychotherapists
120 West Heath Road
London NW3 1LT
Tel: (020) 8458 1609

Association of Cognitive Analytic Therapists
Guy's Hospital
St Thomas's Street
London SE1 9RT
Tel: (020) 7955 5000

Association of Women Psychotherapists
10 Golders Rise
London NW4 2HR
Tel: (020) 8202 0816

British Association for Counselling (BAC)
1 Regent Place
Rugby CV21 2PJ
Tel: (01788) 578328
Web: www.counselling.co.uk

British Association of Psychotherapists
37 Mapesbury Road
London NW2 4HJ
Tel: (020) 8452 9823
Web: www.bap-psychotherapy.org

British Association of Social Workers
16 Kent Street
Birmingham B5 6RD
Tel: (0121) 622 3911
Web: www.bas.co.uk

British Psycho-Analytical Society
Byron House
112a Shirland Road
London W9 2EQ
Tel: (020) 756 3500
Web: www.psycho-analysis.org.uk

British Psychological Society
St Andrew's House
48 Princess Road East
Leicester LE1 7DR
Tel: (0116) 254 9568
Web: www.bps.org.uk

Central Council for Education and Training in Social Work
Derbyshire House
St Chad's Street
London WC1H 8AE
(Psychiatric Social Work)
Tel: (020) 7278 2455
Web: www.ccetsw.org.uk

Clearing House for Postgraduate Courses in Clinical
Psychology
University of Leeds
15 Hyde Terrace
Leeds LS2 9LT
Tel: (0113) 243 1751

Foundation for Psychotherapy and Counselling
607 The Chandlery
Westminster Bridge Road
London SE1 7QY
Tel: (020) 7721 7660
Web: www.therapy-fpc@demon.co.uk

Institute of Psycho-analysis
Byron House
112a–114 Shirland Road
Maida Vale
London W9 2EQ
Tel: (020) 7563 5000
Web: www.psychoanalysis.org.uk

Institute of Psychotherapy & Social Studies
18 Laurier Road
London NW5 1SG
Tel: (020) 7284 4762

MIND (National Association for Mental Health)
Granta House
Broadway
London E15 4BQ
Tel: (020) 8519 2122
Web: www.mind.org.uk

The Psychotherapy Centre
1 Wythburn Place
London W1H 5WL
Tel: (020) 7723 6173

Society of Analytical Psychology
1 Daleham Gardens
London NW3 5BY
Tel: (020) 7435 7696
Web: www.jungian-analysis.org

United Kingdom Council for Psychotherapy
167–169 Great Portland Street
London W1 5FB
Tel: (020) 7436 3002
Web: www.psychotherapy.org.uk

10 Useful publications

Books

BMJ (1998) *The New Learning Medicine*, BMJ Books, London

Brown, L (1994) *Working in Complementary and Alternative Medicine*, Kogan Page, London

Brown, L (1999) *Teach Yourself Alternative Medicine*, Hodder & Stoughton, London

Ruston, J (1996) *Getting Into Medical School*, Trotman, Richmond

UCAS, *University and College Entrance: Official Guide 2001*, UCAS, London

UCAS, *A Student's Guide to Entry into Medicine*, available from UCAS, Rosehill, New Barn Lane, Cheltenham, Gloucestershire GL52 3LZ

Journals

British Dental Journal
British Journal of General Practice
British Medical Journal
Guardian (on Wednesdays for jobs in social work and mental health)
Health Service Journal
Journal of Public Health Policy
The Lancet

Index

add(s) = address(es)